SUPERWAHLJAHR:
THE GERMAN ELECTIONS IN 1994

SUPERWAHLJAHR:
THE GERMAN ELECTIONS
IN 1994

Edited by
Geoffrey K. Roberts

Routledge
Taylor & Francis Group

LONDON AND NEW YORK

First published in 1996 by Frank Cass & Co. Ltd.

Published 2014 by Routledge

2 Park Square, Milton Park, Abingdon, Oxfordshire OX14 4RN

711 Third Avenue, New York, NY 10017

First issued in paperback 2014

Routledge is an imprint of the Taylor & Francis Group,
an informa business

Copyright © 1995 Frank Cass & Co. Ltd

British Library Cataloguing in Publication Data

Superwahljahr:German Elections in 1994
   I. Roberts, Geoffrey K.
   324.9430879

   ISBN 978-0-714-64682-4 (hbk)

   ISBN 978-1-138-87465-7 (pbk)

Library of Congress Cataloging-in-Publication Data

Superwahljahr : the German elections in 1994 / edited by Geoffrey K. Roberts
   p.   cm.
Includes bibliographical references.
ISBN 978-0-714-64682-4 (hbk)
   1. Elections–Germany. 2. Germany. Bundestag–Elections, 1994.
   3. Germany–Politics and government–1990-   I. Roberts, Geoffrey K.
JN3972.A95S87   1995   95-30140
324.943'0879–dc20   CIP.

This group of studies first appeared in a Special Issue of *German Politics*, Vol.4
No.2 (August 1995), [*Superwahljahr*: The German Elections in 1994].

Contents

Introduction

GEOFFREY K. ROBERTS

The advent of *Superwahljahr* 1994 offered a myriad of opportunities for political scientists, opinion pollsters, commentators and critics to study and analyse the 18 elections scheduled for that year. From the Niedersachsen Land election on 13 March to 16 October (the day of the Bundestag election, three Länder elections and the Nordrhein-Westfalen local council elections) seven Sundays were devoted to the European Parliament and the Bundestag elections, seven Länder elections, and nine sets of local government elections. In that 32-week period, voters in the Saarland and four of the new Länder were asked to vote four times, and in all the other Länder except Hesse, Hamburg, Bremen, Brandenburg and Berlin three times. Add to that list the election in May of a new Federal President, and it is obvious that 1994 was a remarkable year for students of German elections and parties, as well as for the parties, politicians and voters.

This collection is devoted to analysis of those elections: in particular, the Bundestag election, though the campaigning and the results of other elections were often significant in themselves, and were always important as the context in which the Bundestag election campaign took place. The collection includes articles by contributors from Germany and from Britain, from those in universities and from those in other institutions. It was decided to analyse the elections thematically, rather than to focus on specific elections or on the parties separately, though an exception was made for the Party of Democratic Socialism (PDS), since that party is a relatively new, and certainly exotic, participant in German elections, and its electoral successes or failures would affect the fortunes of other parties and could limit the range of prospective coalitions which might result from an election.

The elections in *Superwahljahr* need to be seen in relation both to the historical development of parties and elections in the Federal Republic, and to the more immediate context of the four-year period since reunification and the first all-German Bundestag election on 2 December 1990, including the problems which the parties have encountered since then. This 'scene-setting' is provided by the opening article by Geoffrey Roberts, who – in explaining the unusual degree of uncertainty about the result of the Bundestag election – identifies the historical and institutional features which have tended to make many election-night outcomes in the past unexciting and unsurprising.

Wolfgang Gibowski analyses the ways in which issues in the election, images of the chancellor-candidates and changes in the social composition of voter profiles of parties accounted for the outcome of the election. Carsten Zelle assesses the relative importance of chancellor-candidate images, political issues and party loyalty for explaining voter behaviour in the 1994 Bundestag election, and what happens when 'dissonance' occurs for a voter who, for example, may prefer a chancellor-candidate of one party but the programme of another.

It was to be expected that voting behaviour and party organisation in the new Länder would still differ remarkably from those in the old Länder. Stephen Padgett examines these factors in an article based on his recent research into party organisation in the former German Democratic Republic. He finds a process of electoral concentration at work in the new Länder, greater polarisation there than in the old Länder, and a different, more open 'political market' in east Germany: all of which affect the party system as a whole.

Of course, the astonishing persistence of the PDS in the new Länder allows voters there an option which voters in west Germany also had, but were unlikely to make use of. Jens Bastian explains why the PDS has confounded the prophets who predicted its decline or demise after the 1990 Bundestag election, discusses its search for a role in the party system, and assesses its prospects for the future.

Like 'Superwahljahr', the word 'Politikverdrossenheit' has been a modish term recently, and there were anxieties early in 1994 that the trend away from the established parties and away from electoral participation might intensify.[1] The work of Michael Eilfort is among the most significant and authoritative empirical analyses of this phenomenon. In his article, he identifies various 'myths' associated with the argument about Politikverdrossenheit, and identifies reasons for the relatively recent upsurge in electoral abstentionism.

From one perspective, successful electoral campaigning is a matter of marketing. Bernhard Boll describes the campaign strategies of the parties in relation to the Bundestag elections, identifies a continuing trend towards increased personalisation of the campaign, notes the invasion of electronic communication into the arena of party publicity, intra-party communication and propaganda, and describes the ways in which the differences between the old and the new Länder make it difficult for parties to present a homogeneous campaign in the Bundestag election.

What does it all add up to? Peter Pulzer sees the 1994 Bundestag election as possessing elements of continuity and change. If the 1990 election was (as that of 1949 had also been) both the last election of an old regime and the first of a new one, then the Bundestag election of 1994 has continued the transformation from the 'Bonn Republic' to the 'Berlin Republic'. Obviously, as more data becomes available, as the results of the 1994 elections are more intensively analysed, and as the passage of time allows for more reflection, other assessments of *Superwahljahr* will be produced. It is hoped that this special issue will contribute to the process of informing readers about what in some ways has been a uniquely significant set of elections and a party system which is clearly undergoing change.

I wish to express my thanks to the contributors for agreeing to participate in this special issue, and for their prompt delivery of manuscripts. I wish also to thank Stephen Padgett and Gordon Smith for their advice and assistance. I am especially grateful to Kay Green, Hilary Hewitt, Karen Loo and Pauline Sutcliffe for their skilled and cheerful help in preparation of this issue, and to the Manchester Computer Centre staff for their expert assistance.

NOTES

1. Birgit Hoffmann-Jaberg and Dieter Roth, 'Die Nichtwähler. Politische Normalität oder wachsende Distanz zu den Parteien?', in Wilhelm Bürklin and Dieter Roth (eds.), *Das Superwahljahr, Deutschland vor unkalkulierbaren Regierungsmehrheiten?* (Köln, Bund-Verlag, 1994), pp.132–59.

Superwahljahr 1994 and its Effects on the German Party System

GEOFFREY K. ROBERTS

The Bundestag election of 1994 took place in an unusual context: that of 'Superwahljahr' and was the most exciting in terms of uncertainty that there had been for at least 25 years. The causes of the lack of electoral uncertainty in the history of the Federal Republic are analysed. The reasons for this uncertainty: historical, institutional and party-political, are explored in this article.

The Bundestag Election 1994: Journey into the Unknown

Every Bundestag election in Germany is different: different with respect to the political, economic and social context of the campaign; different with regard to the chancellor-candidates (only once has the same pairing of chancellor-candidates contested two elections: Adenauer and Ollenhauer in 1953 and 1957); different in relation to the fortunes of various parties; and so on. Nevertheless, few Bundestag elections have culminated in the degree of tension and excitement provoked by the uncertainty of the outcome such as was the case in 1994. Such uncertainty, to be regarded as significant, must apply to at least one of two aspects of the election result. There can be uncertainty about the party composition of the government to be formed after the election: only the elections of 1949, 1957 and 1969 can properly be placed in that category.[1] In 1953 and 1965 it was reasonably certain that a CDU–CSU and FDP coalition would continue in office, and in 1961 that this coalition would be re-created. In the elections of 1972, 1976 and 1980 there was little possibility of anything other than a continuation of the SPD–FDP coalition; in 1983, 1987 and 1990 it was clear in advance that the CDU–CSU and FDP coalition would continue after each of those elections. Secondly (and of little importance unless simultaneously affecting the party composition of the government), there might be uncertainty about which parties retained (or regained) representation in the Bundestag, or else secured it for the first time. In this case, the elections of 1949, 1953, 1969 and 1990 are the only significant cases prior to 1994.[2]

The 1994 Bundestag election was the first since 1969 to fall into both categories of uncertainty. Up to the day of the election, there was a significant degree of uncertainty concerning the party composition of the government which might emerge after the election, and – closely linked to that uncertainty – there was some doubt about the continued presence in the Bundestag of the FDP and PDS (for the PDS, in terms at least of the number of constituency victories it would achieve and hence about whether it would obtain a proportional distribution of list seats in addition to its constituency seats), as well as about the re-entry of the Greens.[3] Arithmetic was the factor which linked these two types of uncertainty.

(a) If the FDP did not return to the Bundestag then it was unlikely that the CDU–CSU could govern except in a grand coalition. Its run of poor results in local and Länder elections and in the nationwide European Parliament election suggested that it might well fail to obtain the necessary five per cent of the total vote, and a survey in September found that 57 per cent of respondents thought that the FDP would not return to the Bundestag (37 per cent thought it would retain its representation).[4] Except in the unlikely event of a two-party Bundestag, the Christian Democrats would very probably not have sufficient seats to govern alone. However, if the FDP did return to the Bundestag, then it was very probable that the CDU–CSU and FDP coalition would continue in office.

(b) If the PDS retained its membership in the Bundestag and managed to win at least three constituencies (thus evading the five per cent requirement for a proportional distribution of list seats) further complications could arise. The arithmetic might require a grand coalition to be formed (especially if the FDP failed to return to the Bundestag), since the SPD had specifically excluded the possibility of governing by means of PDS voting support.

(c) If the Greens failed to return to the Bundestag (and local and Länder election results in East Germany had been extremely disappointing for them), this would only be significant if the FDP also failed to retain Bundestag representation. Then if the PDS were present in significant numbers, a 'nightmare scenario' of a grand coalition with the PDS as the sole opposition party might result (that is if the Christian Democrats had fewer seats than the SPD plus the PDS). If the PDS were not present, or had only one or two seats, then a single-party government of the Christian Democrats would be formed.

The evidence of opinion polls, supplementing the run of local and Länder elections and the European Parliament election which had taken place in late 1993 and 1994, indicated that nothing could be regarded as settled in advance of election day.

Such complexity and uncertainty on election night is a new phenomenon since 1969. The growing sophistication of opinion polls and exit polls, combined with the invariable practice since 1969 of the FDP indicating well in advance of the election campaign that it would seek to continue in government with its existing coalition partner, meant that hardly anyone had expected the Christian Democrats to displace Brandt in 1972 or Helmut Schmidt in 1976 or 1980. After the 1982–83 '*Wende*', there was no serious possibility by the time election day arrived that Vogel, Rau or Lafontaine would take away the chancellorship from Helmut Kohl.

Why, then, this change in 1994? Any explanation needs to examine the historical, institutional and political factors which have made the 1994 Bundestag election so different from its recent predecessors.

Historical Factors

One reason for the previous lack of uncertainty concerning Bundestag election outcomes has been the rapid development after the war of a three-party system in the Federal Republic. This, combined with the inability of either of the two large parties (the Christian Democrats and the Social Democrats) to secure an overall majority of seats alone, except in the 1957 election, established a pattern whereby almost invariably the FDP was necessary as a coalition partner to provide a majority for the government.[5]

The party constellation which developed in West Germany after 1945 was shaped by the licensing provision of the occupation regime and by the potent memories of the failings and frailties of the party system of the Weimar Republic. By the time of the founding of the Federal Republic, parties had worked together in elected legislatures at Land and local government levels, and in the Economic Council in Frankfurt and the Parliamentary Council in Bonn. The major issue for the parties was: how much or how little should socialist ideas shape the policies of the Federal Republic? Where the Christian Democrats displayed some ambiguity or even some degree of sympathy regarding socialist policies, right-wing liberals seized the initiative (as in Hesse). Some liberals were seduced by the idea of creating a 'national anti-socialist rally' which would combine Christian Democrats, Liberals, Conservatives and nationalists within one electoral organisation. In Hamburg, for instance, electoral alliances of the CDU, FDP and German Party (DP) were successful in replacing the SPD in power for a while.[6] However, this scheme for a right-wing 'rally' came to nothing. Instead, a party system in which there were five relevant parties developed after 1949: the SPD, the Communists (KPD), the Christian Democrats, the liberal FDP and the German Party (DP). Regionally important or issue-based parties managed to win some seats only in the first two Bundestag elections.

Three factors especially contributed to the formation of a three-party Bundestag by 1961. Perhaps the most important of these was the electoral system. The system of proportional representation combined with single-member constituencies invented by the Parliamentary Council (with the advice and consent of the occupying powers) for the 1949 Bundestag election was modified twice – in advance of the 1953 and 1957 elections – in such a way as to increase the difficulties of small parties seeking to qualify for seats in the Bundestag.[7] The 1956 Electoral Law, unchanged in its fundamental provisions, has applied to all Bundestag elections since 1957.[8] A key provision of the Electoral Law is that parties must obtain at least five per cent of votes for party lists (or, instead, win three constituency seats) to qualify for an allocation of seats on the basis of proportional representation. This meant that by 1961 only the FDP retained Bundestag representation alongside the SPD and the Christian Democrats, and that only the Greens (in 1983 and 1987) since then had managed to overcome that five per cent hurdle. Not since 1957 had a party qualified for list seats by securing three constituency seats instead of five per cent of list votes.

Indeed, the constituencies won by the FDP and the PDS in east Germany in 1990 were the only constituency seats that had not been won by either the SPD or the CDU–CSU since the 1957 election.[9]

The second factor was the rapidly evolved facility of the Christian Democrats, and then, with the process which culminated in the Godesberg programme of 1959, the Social Democrats, to act as *Volksparteien* (roughly: 'catch-all parties'),[10] able to appeal to voters beyond the traditional milieux of the church (especially the Catholic church) and the trade unionised working class. This development had two closely related consequences. It made redundant parties such as the Centre Party, the German Party and (even before its prohibition by the constitutional court) the KPD, because all but the most loyal voters for those parties could find in those *Volksparteien* an acceptable party for which to vote. Secondly, where such minor parties survived, they found it increasingly difficult to approach, let alone to surpass, the five per cent barrier to entry to the Bundestag and the Land legislatures; so even those voters still prepared to vote for them out of loyalty or political preference might be dissuaded from doing so by the 'wasted vote' argument so familiar to third-party voters in British elections.

Third – far less important, though – was the provision of Article 21 of the Basic Law which allowed the constitutional court to prohibit anti-democratic parties. Though only two parties: the extreme right-wing Socialist Reich party (SRP) in 1952 and the KPD 1956, were prohibited by the court (and both had by those dates of prohibition become already insignificant in terms of national electoral politics), the existence of that constitutional sanction reinforced the trend towards three-party politics.

So, until 1994, and even allowing for potential coalition complications because of the Greens' presence in the Bundestag, elections to the Bundestag were almost invariably about confirming the existing coalition in government (and it is noteworthy in this respect that the only exception to this confirmation process occurred in 1969, following a 'grand coalition'), and about indicating rises or declines in support especially for the Christian Democrats and the Social Democrats.

Institutional Factors

Two institutional factors have contributed to the unusual nature of the 1994 Bundestag election.

The Bundestag election took place at the end of the series of elections that had provoked the application of the term: '*Superwahljahr*' (super-election year) to 1994. This series included the election to the European Parliament and elections to the Länder legislatures in Niedersachsen, Bayern, Saarland and the five new Länder, as well as local government elections in several of the Länder. Though, in addition to local elections in Nordrhein-Westfalen, the Länder elections in Thüringen, Mecklenburg-Vorpommern and Saarland took place on the same day as the Bundestag election, that did mean that in those regions the Bundestag election campaign itself was overlaid by, or at least mixed in with, Länder election issues. This concentration of elections (to which was added the politically controversial election of the Federal president in May) will probably not occur in quite that intensity again for many years.[11] It has, though, had at least two consequences. One is the probability that voters – at least in those Länder whose Land elections also occurred in 1994 – became weary of elections and electioneering (some having been called upon to vote in four elections in 1994), which might have affected turnout and the choices made by those voters who did go to the polls on 16 October.[12] The second consequence is that the results of earlier elections – especially the poor showing of the FDP and the local strength of the PDS – might have had 'bandwagon' or 'underdog' effects on voting choice in the Bundestag election.

The other institutional factor concerned the extension of the electorate as a consequence of reunification. True: this was not the first, but the second, 'all-German' election. The 1990 election, however, was exceptional in two important respects. It occurred in the extraordinary atmosphere of optimism and jubilation that had followed the act of reunification, two months earlier, and voting choices in the new Länder of east Germany in particular had more to do with the spirit of the times than with longer lasting party sympathies or carefully considered voting decisions. It also made use of a temporary variation of the Federal Republic's electoral system, so that parties qualified for list seats (and qualified in both east and west Germany) by securing five per cent of 'second' votes in either east or west Germany.[13] The 1994 election marked a reversion to normality in both respects. The euphoria of reunification had long since evaporated, though of course problems of reunification remained relevant to party campaigning and to voter choices. Party identification in east Germany had not developed to anything like the extent to which it existed – still – in west Germany. Also, parties now required – as in the pre-1990 period – five per cent of all second votes or, what became once again after many decades a relevant part of the Electoral Law, three constituency victories in order to obtain a proportional allocation of seats.

Political Factors

Election campaigns take place within historical and institutional contexts; they also are affected by the political context of the time. Whilst numerous different political events and developments had occurred in the years since the 1990 Bundestag election and which in some way affected the party system, the most salient will be discussed here.

One obvious factor was the differential development which had occurred in east and west Germany. It would be too unsubtle to say that a prosperous west Germany had suffered from taxation and public debt burdens to subsidise the economy of a shattered east Germany, but that would indicate perhaps the west German perception of the situation. At first, the west German economy had benefited from reunification: the sudden flow of spending power of east German citizens following economic and monetary union in July 1990; the urgent need for investment in east Germany; the opportunities for banks, retail stores, publishing chains, automobile suppliers, travel agencies and many other businesses to establish themselves in the new Länder: these and other economic developments boosted the west German economy. But the dismantling of east German businesses which were unprofitable in a competitive market situation, the take-overs by western firms of east German enterprises through Treuhand agency sales, the unrealistic levels of east German wage rates (even though they were still below those of west Germany) and other factors all led rapidly to a situation where the gap between the economies and unemployment levels of the two parts of Germany was large and increasing. The – perhaps utopian – hopes of east Germany citizens that, within a year or two, they would have 'caught-up' with the living standards of west Germany were soon revealed as totally unrealistic, and the disappointment and feeling of inequitable treatment which resulted were to play a significant role in voting behaviour in 1994.[14] High unemployment rates and anxieties even among the employed that they might lose their jobs, increasing levels of rents and concern about west German claims to property in which east Germans had lived for decades, declining levels of free social services such as childcare facilities, loss of status (especially those formerly in state or party employment), 'witch-hunts' of those suspected of Stasi connections, and a general feeling of colonisation by west Germany all created a mood within the new Länder that there was a growing gap between the two parts of Germany.[15]

This had two effects on the party system and electoral choices: one particular and one general. The particular effect was disenchantment on the part of east Germans with the parties of the Bonn coalition and with Kohl, the 'chancellor of unification'. Government promises about 'flourishing landscapes' being created in east Germany were seen to have been hollow. Levels of opinion poll support for the Christian Democrats and Free Democrats declined rapidly and sharply.[16] The more general effect was a sense of alienation from the established, western parties. Membership levels of those parties in east Germany declined swiftly (though, compared to membership levels in 1990, also for reasons other than disappointment or alienation), and support grew for alternative parties or movements: for the extreme right, for the PDS and for the idea of an 'east German party'. Whilst support for the extreme right failed to coalesce into party membership or voting support, support for the PDS did stabilise, then increase. It did so especially after attempts to form an east German 'resentment' party failed. Opinion polls had suggested that there was considerable support among east Germans for such a party. Talks between Gregor Gysi (PDS leader) and a 'maverick' east German Christian Democrat, Peter-Michael Diestel (formerly Minister of the Interior in the de Maiziere government, and who had transferred from the German Social Union (DSU) to the CDU) led to the establishment in June 1992 of 'Committees for Justice' (*Gerechtigkeitkomitees*). However, these committees proved to be little more than a 'front' for the PDS, and anyway they eschewed any form of party activity.[17]

In west Germany, the perceived competence and trustworthiness of the government were damaged by the measures it had to impose to finance the consequences of reunification. The so-called 'tax lie': the indication in the 1990 election campaign that reunification could be financed without additional taxation, was a charge which hurt the coalition parties. Controversies over the treatment of asylum-seekers, insurance against invalidity in old age, the deployment of German troops outside the NATO area and the seemingly inexorable rise in crime all contributed to a weakening of the reputation of the government, and of the chancellor. Not until 1994, and more especially mid-1994, did the government and Helmut Kohl recover levels of opinion poll support to any significant degree.

Besides these problems, the established parties confronted other political problems in the period 1991–94. The CDU suffered, like other parties, from a declining and ageing membership. It was a predominantly male party (the proportion of female members in the old Länder was 23.5 per cent, in the new Länder 36.3 per cent[18]). Its leadership was also a problem. Kohl had seemingly ensured that no rival to his leadership could emerge, and, in the process, had restricted the influence of those who wished to reform the party, such as former General-Secretary Geissler and those staff members at party headquarters in Bonn who were sympathetic to Geissler's ideas. Kohl had shaped for the CDU an identity as a conservative right-wing party, but not one sufficiently far on the right either to render superfluous more radical parties such as the Republicans or to make them acceptable coalition partners for the CDU. The party's Christian milieu was in decline, reducing its pool of loyal voters who would support the party through thick and thin. In Land elections after the 1990 Bundestag election, the CDU lost vote-share in ten Länder (in three of those losing over nine per cent) and increased its vote-share in only Bremen, Schleswig-Holstein, Sachsen and Saarland. In the old Länder, it was in government only in Bayern and Baden-Württemberg (and there in a grand coalition, as it was also in Berlin). In the new Länder, the 1994 run of elections left it in government in Sachsen (on its own) and (though as a partner in grand coalitions) in Thüringen and Mecklenburg-Vorpommern.

In the new Länder, the party continued to be troubled by conflicts between the 'old-guard', who had been members of the CDU when it was a socialist ally of the SED, and 'renewers', who wanted to purge the party of its pre-1990 past and make it a democratic partner to the CDU of west Germany. These conflicts had the effect of discouraging the minority of 'renewers' in the party and repelling potential members who did not wish to be associated with politicians whom, perhaps, they had known in the pre-1990 period as beneficiaries of the block-party system. Attempts led by Volker Rühe (then the CDU General Secretary) to support the replacement of the 'old guard' by 'renewers' found little support in the Länder parties in east Germany; even Kurt Biedenkopf, chairman of the Sachsen CDU, said that Rühe's attacks on long-standing CDU members were too undifferentiated.[19]

A series of scandals and charges of corruption of various kinds also damaged the CDU–CSU. In Bavaria the 'Amigo' scandal led to the replacement of minister-president Max Streibl by Edmund Stoiber in 1993. Lothar Späth had to resign as minister-president of Baden-Württemberg in

1991 because of a similar scandal. In the new Länder, the minister-presidents of Thüringen, Sachsen-Anhalt (twice) and Mecklenburg-Vorpommern, as well as the CDU Land chairman in Sachsen and Thüringen, all had to resign for various reasons concerning scandal or political ill-judgement. Two east German ministers in the Bonn cabinet (Krause and de Maiziere) resigned because of scandal and suspected Stasi links, respectively.

One potential threat to the CDU, electoral competition from the DSU, came to nothing, however, because the DSU forced the CSU to end its patronage of the party. Ideas which the CSU might have had of compensating for its reduced post-reunification political influence by 'expansion by proxy' in the new Länder, using the DSU, thus were never put to the test. The DSU never appeared likely to establish itself as a successful party in the new Länder (let alone extend to west German Länder, as it threatened to do). However, any votes which it attracted, especially in Länder elections, would probably have been at the expense of the CDU, so the CDU was not prepared to see its Bonn ally, the CSU, subsidise and assist it.

While the SPD did not suffer from the legacy of 'old guard' members in east Germany, it had what was almost a worse problem: shortage of members of any kind in the new Länder. Membership levels in the new Länder were derisory, compared either to pre-Hitler levels or to levels attained by the PDS. The party in east Germany was only slowly attracting working-class members to a party which had been formed and developed by intellectuals and members of the professions. So many of those members were office-holders, either within the party or on public bodies, that they had little time for recruitment activities. There was lack of agreement within the party about the attitude to take to former SED members wishing to join the SPD. Some – such as Wolfgang Thierse – were inclined to allow admission to such applicants, if necessary with safeguards about their past histories and conditions under which they could hold office in the SPD. Others took a more sceptical view, concerned that such former communists could swamp local branches and damage the image of the SPD.[20] An article in Vorwärts in 1992 summarised the arguments for and against admission.[21]

The party also had leadership problems. Having tried three different chancellor-candidates without success in the period since the displacement of the Schmidt government in 1982 (Vogel, Rau, Lafontaine), and having a vacancy in the party chairmanship when Vogel resigned in December 1990, the party turned to the minister-president of Schleswig-Holstein, Björn Engholm, to fill both positions. However, he resigned from all his public and party offices as a consequence of revelations concerning the truthfulness of his evidence to a committee of inquiry into the Barschel affair, and so a replacement had to be found. The party adopted an imaginative device to choose its chairman in 1993: a ballot of the membership. Rudolf Scharping, minister-president of Rheinland-Pfalz, was chosen, and was confirmed later by the party conference.[22] Scharping then became the chancellor-candidate of the SPD.

The SPD had to find a policy platform which could do three (possibly mutually incompatible) things: unite the party; win voting support in both the old and the new Länder for the European, local and Land elections, as well as the Bundestag election; and prove sufficiently flexible to accommodate any of a variety of coalition possibilities: particularly coalition with the Greens, possibly (as in Bremen) with the Greens and the FDP, even (as in Baden-Württemberg) with the CDU. This led to a certain blandness and lack of detail in the policy pronouncements and electoral manifestos that were produced in 1994. The principal television party political broadcast, for instance, focusing on Scharping's own family background and political beliefs, suggested pictorially that all was very well with Germany and with the Scharping household, but the somewhat incompatible verbal message conveyed was that Germany's situation was so bad that a change of government was vitally necessary.

The SPD's situation was made worse because it was competing for the centre ground with the FDP and Christian Democrats to its right, but on its left it had to compete against the resurgent Greens in west Germany (less so in the new Länder), but the PDS in east Germany. This made it difficult to adjust policy pronouncements to the two parts of Germany without being trapped into saying different things to the two different electorates.

But the principal problem for the SPD concerned its attitude to the PDS. Relying on authoritative forecasts that the PDS would not continue to exist as a Bundestag party after the electoral system reverted to normal in 1994, the SPD only awoke to the strategic problem posed by the electoral successes of the PDS after the Berlin local elections in 1992, confirmed by successes in local elections in Brandenburg at the end of 1993. Decisions by the Bonn leadership to rule out any sort of co-operation with the PDS seemed to be clear enough. However, this line was not always regarded sympathetically in the SPD in the new Länder, and the situation became more complicated when the results of the Sachsen-Anhalt Land election in June became known. The only alternative to a grand coalition was a minority government of the SPD and Alliance 90–Greens, and the minister-president of such an administration presumably would need PDS votes to be elected by the Landtag. That was the choice which the Sachsen-Anhalt SPD made, but it immediately offered the CDU–CSU and the FDP a weapon with which to attack the SPD in the Bundestag and other Landtag election campaigns. The 'Magdeburg model' was thrown at Scharping time and time again in the campaign, despite his insistence that he would not allow himself to be elected as chancellor if PDS votes in the Bundestag were needed to give him a majority. There were moral, political and pragmatic reasons for keeping the PDS at arm's length (whilst hoping to persuade voters sympathetic to the PDS to vote SPD).[23] Memories of the forced fusion of the SPD with the Communist party in East Germany, and the unreadiness of the PDS to admit that it had been a *forced* fusion, were further reasons for not entertaining ideas about some kind of new 'popular front'.[24] Though some in the east German SPD tried to make a plausible case for some united left-wing party activity involving the PDS, the 'Dresden Declaration' of 11 August 1994 contained a clear decision by the SPD Executive to rule out a strategy of alliance with the PDS, calling it a 'party of inconsequential populist promises' which had yet to make a clean break with its communist past.[25]

The FDP managed for some time to hold on in opinion polls to the high levels of support which it had obtained in the 1990 Bundestag election. An Allensbach poll in May 1992, for example, showed that 11.1 per cent in west Germany and 13.9 per cent in east Germany supported the FDP.[26] However, the resignation in April 1992 of Genscher as Foreign Minister removed the best known of the FDP's leading politicians (and one of the most admired of German political figures) from the stage, and with Lambsdorff's retirement as party leader in 1993 the party suffered the loss of another well known senior figure. A series of unhappy contests for various political offices had begun even in the aftermath of the 1990 election, involving ministerial posts and the leadership of the parliamentary party group, and continued with the contest for the vacant foreign ministry (Frau Schwaetzer being nominated by the party leadership, but defeated by Klaus Kinkel, the Justice Minister, in a vote by the parliamentary party group and party executive committee). When Jürgen Möllemann had to resign in January 1993 as Minister of Economic Affairs following a minor scandal, his successor, Günter Rexrodt, was appointed after an uncontroversial but contested election by the parliamentary group and executive committee. However, another mishap occurred in February 1994 following the resignation of Rainer Ortleb as Minister for Education and Science. The nomination of Wolfgang Gerhardt, the Hesse FDP leader, was unfortunately announced to the press before the parliamentary party and executive committee had agreed to it, and in a contested election Gerhardt was narrowly defeated by Karl-Heinz Laermann. This affair embarrassed both the party's leadership and the chancellor. These changes also left the FDP with a collection of inexperienced ministers in the cabinet. With the elimination of Möllemann as a credible candidate for the party leadership, Kinkel was elected at the 1993 party congress. However, he had only been a party member since January 1991, and his leadership skills were untried.

Criticism mounted regarding his leadership, and doubts were expressed about his ability to handle simultaneously the leadership of the party and the onerous burdens of being Foreign Minister (especially in 1994, when Germany held the presidency of the Council of Ministers of the European Union). Several policy issues, where the FDP seemed to demonstrate uncertainty or division concerning what line it should take (on asylum law, use of German troops for United Nations peacekeeping efforts, compulsory old-age invalidity insurance, for instance) further damaged the party's image.

By early 1994, opinion poll support for the party had declined markedly. An Allensbach poll published in April gave the party 8.2 per cent, for instance.[27] The party had failed to nurture its east German branches, and membership there dropped rapidly. Commencing with the Hamburg Land election in September 1993, the party experienced an unprecedented series of electoral defeats. In nine successive Land elections – including those held on the same day as the Bundestag election – and in the European Parliament election, it failed to obtain the five per cent of votes needed for representation. Consequently, it approached the Bundestag election campaign with trepidation, realising that it was closer to exclusion from the Bundestag than ever before. Only a successful 'second-vote' campaign, which would draw support from Christian Democrat sympathisers, could save it.[28]

The PDS at the end of 1990 seemed to be the party least likely to prosper in the coming four years. Its problems were legion, and experts predicted a rapid decline for the party. Moreau, writing in 1992, said: 'The decline of this party seems inevitable in the short term'.[29] The conflicts with the Treuhand and the Independent Commission on Party Property over what the PDS could legally retain in the way of wealth and property; the scandals about improper diversion of its funds to foreign bank accounts; disclosures about links of PDS politicians to the Stasi; trials of former SED leaders: these seemed to be blackening the reputation of the party irretrievably. The PDS had failed to decide upon a clear political identity for itself, and still harboured a 'Communist Platform', which weakened the credibility of the claim of the PDS to be a 'new' socialist party, rather than the SED in a new guise. Membership of the PDS was in decline, and what members remained tended to be ageing, unreconstructed former SED members (95 per cent of PDS members had been members of the SED). By March 1994 only 131,000 members remained in the party; in June 1991 it had been 242,000.[30] The likelihood of the SPD and the Greens by the 1994 elections eroding the electoral support of the PDS seemed high, especially as the recovery of the east German economy took hold. The party failed to make any progress in establishing itself as a credible force in west Germany.

Yet by the start of *Superwahljahr* its situation was almost unrecognisably different. It had had encouraging results in local elections in Berlin in 1992 (29.7 per cent in east Berlin districts), and in Brandenburg at the end of 1993 (21.2 per cent). In local elections in the other new Länder in June 1994 it polled between 15.7 and 24.3 per cent. In the Sachsen-Anhalt, Brandenburg and Sachsen Länder elections it obtained between 16.5 and 19.9 per cent. It only just failed to get five per cent nationwide in the European Parliament election in June.

This recovery was attributable to two factors. Government policy and economic development had not produced swiftly enough the 'flourishing landscape' in east Germany which Kohl had promised, so many people in east Germany saw themselves as 'losers' or were worried that they might become 'losers' from the reunification process. This was reinforced by feelings of resentment among many east Germans, because of uncertainties about housing and employment, growing criminality, what they perceived as 'colonial' arrogance of west German businessmen, officials, politicians, and teachers, the undiminished gap in living standards between the two parts of Germany, and even the interminable series of court cases and investigations concerning the crimes of the former regime. The PDS offered a sense of pride, or at least of justification to people who had come to reject the idea that democracy was the best form of government.[31] The second factor was the inability of the SPD to establish itself in east Germany, organisationally and in terms of its policies, as the main challenger to the CDU–CSU and FDP. All this left the field open to some form of east German 'resentment' party.[32] The PDS managed to claim this role for itself, in large measure thanks to the political cunning of Gysi, who was able to neutralise attempts to create a new east German party by participating in the creation of the *Gerechtigkeitkomitees*,[33] and managed to keep the different factions in the party together and resist claims of the Treuhand concerning PDS finances. He also was popular enough to gain high levels of recognition and acceptance among east German voters. The election of Lothar Bisky as party chairman at the congress held in January 1993 (Gysi had decided to give up the chairmanship) still left Gysi as the *de facto* party leader: he led the PDS Bundestag group, and took the leading role in the election campaigning of 1994.

By early 1994, a survey revealed that 55 per cent of east German respondents considered the PDS to be a renewed and democratic party, which should be in the Bundestag.[34] Its strategy of 'open lists', to attract candidates who were not party members and voters who were not normally PDS sympathisers, was tactfully clever, but also politically adept, since it seemed to give the PDS an image of being pragmatic and non-ideological. The party also benefited from active and committed supporters. Not only was the PDS the party with the most members in east Germany (the CDU had 87,300 and the SPD had only 25,700 members in the new Länder); it was the only party there with a properly functioning and autonomous party organisation, and the only one with *Stammwähler* (a base of loyal voters); these were big advantages in *Superwahljahr*.[35] Nor did it have to conduct an austere campaign: it was still a very wealthy party: the owner of an estimated DM 1.8 billion in property and other wealth.[36]

The Greens began the post-1990 Bundestag election period as the most demoralised of all the main parties. The shock of not returning to the Bundestag in 1990 had hit the west German Greens hard. This had financial, as well as political, consequences: a need for DM 2 million savings was identified at the beginning of 1991. The resources that went with membership of the Bundestag (money for the work of the *Fraktion*, for instance) was lost to the party. The party congress in 1991 at Neumünster was crucial to the fate of the Greens. Here a 'last stand' of the 'fundamentalist' wing took place. Though not all the reforms which the 'realists' wanted to implement at that congress were pushed through, it was clear that the centre of gravity in the party had moved towards the more moderate wing. Jutta Ditfurth and those other 'fundamentalists' who supported her walked out of the Neumünster congress, and in May 1991 held a conference of about 300 sympathisers in Frankfurt to form a new organisation for the 'independent ecological left'. The 'Realos' did succeed in persuading the conference to adopt the 'Declaration of Neumünster', which among other things admitted that the organisation of the party was 'chaotic' and 'undemocratic', and at the second part of the party congress, in Köln in June, other organisational changes, including the election of a 'political business manager' (Heide Rühle), were accepted.[37] By then it was obvious that Dittfurth had not succeeded in tempting away many Green members, any more than Grühl in 1980 or Trampert and Ebermann in 1988 had done.[38]

Encouraging results in the Länder elections (in 1991 and 1992 the party failed to win seats only in Schleswig-Holstein) accompanied moves towards fusion with Alliance 90, the east German citizen-movement organisation, which had become a 'proper' party in September 1991. After long discussions, membership ballots in April 1993 of both parties voted in favour of merger by overwhelming majorities (on turnouts of nearly 50 per cent for the Greens, 60 per cent for Alliance 90) and a conference in Leipzig in May 1993 sealed the merger. Alliance 90 succeeded in securing the name 'Alliance 90/the Greens' for the merged party (with 'the Greens' as the official short form), and won concessions concerning guaranteed representation in the party's leading structures and its rights to retain certain separate structures in east Germany. This merger was not straightforward or conflict-free. Resistance in some of the Länder (especially Brandenburg), and doubts about the compatibility of the policies which each constituent party wished to pursue, existed both before the merger and afterwards, and were to affect the election campaigning of the merged party in *Superwahljahr*.

By 1993, though, the Greens could be confident that they would return to the Bundestag in October 1994. Opinion polls suggested levels of support of between eight and ten per cent. Land elections produced some excellent results: in the re-run Hamburg election in 1993 the party had its best ever Land result: 13.5 per cent; in the Niedersachsen Land election in March 1994 it won 7.4 per cent. In both cases. the Greens made gains compared to the previous election; in both cases, though, it was unable to participate in government. The June election in Sachsen-Anhalt brought a less encouraging result: only 5.1 per cent (though compensated by winning over ten per cent in the European Parliament elections). The Greens did join with the SPD in government in Sachsen-Anhalt, but the coalition needed the votes of the PDS to become the government, and this 'toleration' strategy was seen as a matter for conflict within the Greens (and especially the Alliance 90 section), as it was in the SPD. After all, how could a party which had grown out of the citizen movement of 1989–90 in the GDR now have a relationship with the successor-party to the SED? For some Greens (especially those who still resented reunification) this was no big deal; for some on the left, the PDS seemed a desirable partner, even.[39] But the matter related to more general issues of the relationship of the Greens to the GDR in the past, and to the idea of Germany and the Greens fear of resurgent nationalism in the present.[40] Perhaps because of this problem in Sachsen-Anhalt, in other Länder elections in east Germany the Greens failed to obtain the necessary five per cent (though the party did get over five per cent in Bayern and Saarland). Indeed, poor results in the Brandenburg and Sachsen Länder elections led to rumours of divisions within the party, and fears that perhaps re-entry to the Bundestag would not necessarily be as automatic as was earlier hoped.

'The Greens have had to learn, and still must learn, that the laws of political success in party competition cannot simply be invalidated because they do not want to accept their validity for themselves.'[41] This judgement of Kleinert was relevant to the 1990 Bundestag election result, and by 1994 the party seemed to have learned that lesson. For the first time, the Greens engaged a professional public relations firm to plan and implement its publicity strategy, with a campaign budget which, at DM 5.5 million, was nearly double that for 1990, and for the first time it deliberately encouraged media attention for its 'prominent' politicians. Joschka Fischer especially (but Antje Vollmer and Ludger Volmer also, among others) were presented as the personalities associated with Green policies and Green campaign strategy.[42] The party's Mannheim congress, in February 1994, had adopted an election programme heavily biased towards 'Realo' demands, and had made a positive, if conditional, statement favouring a post-election coalition with the SPD.[43]

The merged party, then, was by no means well integrated as it campaigned in 1994. The merger had been between a much larger, primarily western, Green party and a smaller, almost exclusively east German Alliance 90. 'In the long run, the politics of size is likely to prevail in the new party: unification almost inevitably means western dominance' wrote Poguntke after the merger.[44] It was the fear of western dominance, combined with the weak position of the party in east Germany and the disparate policy orientations, which left the Greens as the least united of the parties contesting the Bundestag election of 1994.

'Freedom includes also the freedom to form parties.'[45] For a short period, extending roughly from the second half of 1993 to the European Parliament election in June 1994, it seemed as though a further complication to the party system might emerge: electoral support for a new party. Opinion polls suggested that support for 'new' parties among an electorate disillusioned with the established parties might be as high as 30 per cent.[46]

Two such new parties did seem to offer a potentially effective challenge to the established parties. The 'STATT party' ('statt' meaning 'instead of'), formed by a breakaway group of CDU members in Hamburg, had an astonishing success in a re-run Land election in Hamburg in 1993.[47] The new party obtained 5.6 per cent of the votes and thus obtained seats in the Hamburg legislature. The CDU, SPD and FDP (which failed to obtain the qualifying five per cent needed to win any seats) all lost vote-share. Electoral support for the new party came from former CDU voters (35 per cent of the STATT party vote) and former SPD voters (27 per cent of the STATT party vote). Because the STATT party did especially well in areas where voters were public-sector employees or white-collar staff, it robbed the FDP of support.[48] Failure of talks between the SPD and the Greens to produce a coalition agreement led to successful negotiations between the SPD and the STATT party; the STATT party would support a SPD-led Land government, and would nominate three members of that government. The novelty of this breakthrough by the new party provoked an immoderate degree of attention by the mass media, and considerable interest in a number of other Länder, where versions of the STATT party started to be formed. In spite of considerable reluctance among some of the leaders of the Hamburg party about extending beyond Hamburg, it was agreed to form a national STATT party (the Hamburg party voted 159–44 on this proposal at a meeting on 22 January 1994) and a first federal party congress was held in Kassel on 26–27 March 1994. Divisions concerning strategy, problems about the legitimacy of some of the Land versions of the party that had formed, lack of substantive political programme that went beyond procedural innovations, personal quarrels and challenges to the legality of office-holders in the federal party, together with fears that the extreme right might attempt to infiltrate the party led to it losing all credibility among the electorate. It could not repeat its Hamburg success either in the Niedersachsen or Sachsen-Anhalt Länder elections (polling 1.3 per cent and 0.3 per cent respectively), and in the European Parliament election it polled only 0.5 per cent (and in that election secured only 1.8 per cent in Hamburg). It did not contest the Bundestag election, and by the end of 1994 it seemed to have faded into irrelevance.

The Bund freier Bürger (BfB: Association of Free Citizens) was the other new party that seemed to have realistic prospects of electoral success. It was formed by Manfred Brunner, a former chairman of the Bavarian FDP and senior staff member of the Commission of the European Community. His critical attitude to the Maastricht Treaty and the prospect of currency union (which had led to the termination of his career in Brussels), and his failure to persuade the Constitutional Court to rule that the Maastricht Treaty was not in conformity with the Basic Law, prompted him and some associates to form this new party at a meeting in Wiesbaden on 23 January 1994. Though it had a programme of policy proposals based primarily on free market principles and the reduction of state interference in the economy, the BfB was basically a single-issue party, concerned with opposing the path of development which the European Union seemed set upon since the Maastricht Treaty. By obtaining only 1.1 per cent of the votes cast in the European Parliament election in June 1994, in an election which the party regarded as a 'test election', it demonstrated that its inexperience and limited message were unable to attract the disaffected FDP and CDU/CSU voters which it had supposed were going to be won over.

The new parties were thus apparently temporary experiments, unable to cause complications in the German party system, but which nevertheless may have caused a proper degree of anxiety within the ranks of the established parties about their continued ability to attract and retain the support of voters.[49]

The parties of the extreme right seemed to play no significant part in the elections of *Superwahljahr*. They had had, once again, a brief period of electoral success in 1991–92 (comparable to that in 1987–89), caused largely by the growing salience of the immigrant/asylum-seeker issue. The Deutsche Volksunion (DVU) again won representation in the Bremen Land parliament in 1991. In 1992 the Republicans achieved a remarkable 10.9 per cent in the Baden-Württemberg Land election, forcing the two big parties to form a 'grand coalition'; on the same day, the DVU polled 6.3 per cent in the Schleswig-Holstein Land election. In Hamburg in 1993 these two extreme right parties shared 7.6 per cent between them, but neither won over five per cent, so neither obtained seats. After that, these parties faded into electoral insignificance, helped by legislation in Bonn to control the influx of asylum-seekers. The Republicans polled over three per cent in Land elections in Niedersachsen and Bayern, but otherwise results tended to be well under two per cent. Efforts to link parties of the extreme right came to nothing. The Deutsche Liga für Volk und Heimat, formed in 1991 by former members of the Republican and National Democratic parties, never gathered enough support to be a serious player in the party game. When it became known that Frey (of the DVU) and Schönhuber (the Republican's leader) were negotiating a kind of 'mutual aid' agreement, it merely hastened Schönhuber's departure and the consequent battle to succeed him in the party.[50] By November 1994, in-fighting in the Republican party threatened its continued existence.[51]

It seems clear that much of the temporary voting support which the extreme right parties could harvest in 1991–92 came from 'protest voters', using this vote as an alternative to abstention.

The Republicans, which profited significantly from the loss of prestige and function of the established parties, themselves offer an image of political apathy and amateurish political inability. It is at best a distorting mirror, not a remedy, for the 'crisis of party'.[52]

Doubtless, such parties will again from time to time be recipients of protest voting, but that in itself seems relatively harmless as a threat to Germany's democracy.

More of the Same?

The elections of *Superwahljahr* will be closely analysed by political scientists, but also by the parties, for each of them is still faced with problems and an uncertain future. The FDP has to try to find a programme, an identity, and a way of recovering electoral support at Land and local levels: the Hesse Land election in 1995 shows that it has at least a chance of doing this. The SPD has to decide on a strategy to return to government: to wait for the FDP to change partners? to hope that the PDS will collapse and leave its east German vote to the SPD? The Greens need to integrate their east German membership, and indeed expand their membership and voting support in east Germany. The PDS has to settle its internal problems, and decide on what kind of party it wants to be: to continue to trade on east German resentments – which may anyway erode over the next four years?

or to plot a programme which would make it a more permanent challenger to the SPD: a 'Godesberg for the PDS', as Bisky and other 'moderates' want?[53] The Christian Democrats must prepare for the coming post-Kohl era. Whoever their new leader will be, problems of adjustment and issues of policy will have to be resolved.

In addition, all the parties will need to respond to issues such as party financing: the new rules simultaneously impose new limits on the parties' income, yet cost the state more than ever: DM 352 million in 1994.[54] Whatever its causes, extent and nature, the growing rejection of parties and of activism within parties by the public is another continuing challenge to the party system.

The party system has not come through either the reunification of Germany or *Superwahljahr* unscathed. It is still in a process of adaptation, in west and east Germany in different ways. It will be fascinating to see what that system looks like in four years' time.

NOTES

1. In 1949 there was uncertainty about the possibility of a 'grand coalition' being formed. In 1957 the uncertainty principally concerned the ability of the CDU–CSU to govern without the FDP, which had left the Adenauer government in 1956. In 1969 the FDP had the choice of forming a coalition with either Brandt's SPD or Kiesinger's CDU–CSU.
2. In 1949 ten parties (and three non-party candidates) were able to obtain seats, thanks to a less rigorous application of limitations to proportional representation. In 1953 only six parties did so. In 1969 there was a strong possibility that the National Democratic Party (NDP) might obtain seats (though it just failed to do so). In 1983 the Greens entered the Bundestag for the first time. In 1990, under a temporary change to the method of calculating seats, the PDS and Alliance '90/the Greens from east Germany secured seats, but – to most people's surprise – the west German Greens did not obtain seats.
3. By the time of the 1994 Bundestag election, the Greens had merged their east German and west German organisations, and this combined party had then in turn merged with Alliance '90.
4. *Der Spiegel*, 19 Sept. 1994, p.22.
5. On the development of the party system, and the changes which have occurred to that system, see Geoffrey K. Roberts, 'Party System Change in West Germany: Land-Federal Linkages', in: Peter Mair and Gordon Smith (eds.), *Understanding Party System Change in Western Europe*, (London: Frank Cass, 1990), pp.98–113.
6. Dieter Hein, *Zwischen liberaler Milieupartei und nationaler Sammlungsbewegung* (Düsseldorf: Droste Verlag, 1985), pp.91–7.
7. Changes in the electoral system and issues of electoral reform are covered in Eckhard Jesse, *Wahlrecht zwischen Kontinuität und Reform. Eine Analyse der Wahlsystemdiskussion und der Wahlrechtsänderungen in der Bundesrepublik Deutschland 1949–1983*, (Düsseldorf: Droste Verlag, 1985).
8. A major exception was the 1990 election, where, as a response to the peculiar situation of the first all-German election since the war and which took place only weeks after formal reunification had occurred, the provisions concerning requirements for distribution of 'lists' seats proportionately to parties were relaxed for that election only. Any party securing five per cent of party-list votes (or, alternatively, winning three constituency seats) in *either* the 'old' Federal Republic *or* in the territory of the former German Democratic Republic

qualified for proportional allocation of seats on an all-German basis.
9. Indeed, in the 1949, 1953 and 1957 elections many of the constituency seats won by small parties (including the FDP in 1949 and 1953) were the consequence of either the CDU–CSU or the SPD agreeing not to present their own candidate (and, in return, having their candidates elsewhere benefiting from the absence of candidates from those allied parties): see Peter Schindler (ed.), *Datenhandbuch zur Geschichte des deutschen Bundestages, 1949–1982* (Bonn: Deutscher Bundestag, 1983), pp.106–9.
10. Gordon Smith, 'The German Volkspartei and the Career of the Catch-all Concept', in H. Döring and G. Smith (eds.), *Party Government and Political Culture in Western Germany,* (London: Macmillan, 1982); Alf Mintzel, *Die Volkspartei, Typus und Wirklichkeit* (Opladen: Westdeutscher Verlag, 1984); Rudolf Wildenmann, *Volksparteien. Ratlose Riesen?* (Baden-Baden: Nomos Verlag, 1989).
11. Some politicians have proposed the introduction of legislation which would require the 'bunching' of election dates to reduce the effect of having a more or less permanent election campaign. Lambsdorff, for example, suggested limiting elections to two Sundays per year, and requiring all Länder legislatures, local councils and the Bundestag to have five-year terms (*Die Welt*, 15 Oct. 1991). This would be difficult to implement, if only because sometimes premature elections become necessary (the Bundestag in 1972 and 1983, for instance, and in Hamburg in 1993). The arguments for and against such imposed scheduling are well set out in: Klaus von Beyme, 'Zusammenlegung von Wahlterminen: Entlassung der Wähler-Entlastung der Politiker?', *Zeitschrift für Parlamentsfragen*, 2 (1992), esp. pp.340–41. Assuming that no such changes are introduced, the next *Superwahljahr* will be in 2014, when again the Bundestag election will coincide with election of the federal president and the European Parliament, the Land legislatures in all the new Länder and in Saarland and Bayern, as well as local elections in many of the Länder.
12. It is interesting to compare the much higher percentages of invalid votes for the Bundestag election in those Länder which had either local or Länder elections simultaneously with the Bundestag election to those of the other Länder. The percentages were: Saarland 3.6; Thüringen 2.4; Mecklenburg-Vorpommern 2.2; Nordrhein-Westfalen 1.9. In all cases these were markedly higher than the equivalent 1990 percentages. The percentages in the other Länder ranged from 1.6 to 0.8. In every 'new' Land except Thüringen and Mecklenburg-Vorpommern, the percentage of invalid votes declined markedly compared to the 1990 Bundestag election figure.
13. Differing from the normal rules, which require either five per cent of 'second' votes in the whole of the Federal Republic – or three constituency victories – to qualify for a proportional distribution of seats.
14. For example, as recently as 1991 two-thirds of east Germans believed that an equalisation of living standards would be attained by 1997; in 1993 only 8 per cent were that optimistic. Increasing numbers of east German citizens were pessimistic about the future in 1993, compared to 1991. (Richard Hilmer and Rita Müller-Hilmer: 'Es wächst zusammen', *Die Zeit*, 1 Oct. 1993).
15. For survey data concerning what east Germans considered to be improvements, and what they considered to have deteriorated, as a result of reunification, see the Allensbach survey published in *Frankfurter Allgemeine Zeitung*, 13 April 1994. Improvements mentioned included the range of goods on offer, freedom to travel and freedom of expression; the negative scores came for rent levels, security against crime and road safety, and issues concerning education and employment.
16. For example, just a year after the 1990 Bundestag election, support in the new Länder had declined to 27.3 per cent for the Christian Democrats, compared to 41.8 per cent in the Bundestag election (Allensbach survey, *Frankfurter Allgemeine Zeitung*, 4 Dec. 1991). In autumn 1993 only 21 per cent of voters in the new Länder said they would vote for the CDU, and 9 per cent for the FDP (Hilmer and Müller-Hilmer, *Die Zeit*, 1 Oct. 1993). This trend continued downwards in early 1994: an Allensbach survey gave the CDU only 19.7 per cent in the new Länder, and the FDP only 8.1 per cent (*Frankfurter Allgemeine Zeitung*, 19 Jan. 1994).
17. On the Gerechtigkeitkomitees, see Heidrun Abromeit, 'Zum Für und Wider einer Ost-Partei',

Gegenwartskunde, vol.41, no.4 (1992), pp.437–48; Patrick Moreau and Viola Neu, *Die PDS zwischen Linksextremismus und Linkspopulismus* (Sankt-Augustin: Konrad Adenauer Stiftung Interne Studien 76/1994), pp.42–5; *Frankfurter Allgemeine Zeitung*, 10 and 13 July 1992; *Der Spiegel*, 5 Oct. 1992, pp.73–5.

18. Josef Schmid, 'Die CDU in Ostdeutschland', *Deutschland Archiv*, Aug. 1994, p.797.
19. *Frankfurter Allgemeine Zeitung*, 30 Aug. 1991.
20. Wolfgang Thierese, 'Wahl '94: was tun?', *Aus Politik und Zeitgeschichte*, 15, 15 April 1994, p.19 and in an interview in *Der Spiegel*, 7 Nov. 1994, pp.23–4; Markus Merkl, 'Bloss keine Nähe', *Die Zeit*, 4 Nov. 1994; *Der Spiegel*, 21 Oct. 1991, p.57.
21. 'Türen auf für alte "Blockfreunde"', *Vorwärts*, January 1992, p.13.
22. Three candidates offered themselves. The vote shares were: Rudolf Scharping 40.23 per cent; Gerhard Schröder (prime minister of Niedersachsen) 33.19 per cent; Heide Wieczoreck-Zeul (Member of the Bundestag and former chair of the Young Socialists) 26.56 per cent. Just over 50 per cent of the membership voted (*Das Parlament*, 18 June 1993).
23. Joachim Raschke, ''SPD und PDS. Selbstblockade oder Opposition?'', *Blätter für deutsche und internationale Politik*, December 1994, pp.1456–63.
24. Ilse Spittmann, 'Neue Kräftekonstellation', *Deutschland Archiv*, December 1994, p.1235.
25. Documents concerning the relationship between the SPD and PDS in: *Blätter für deutsche und internationale Politik*, January 1995, pp.118–123.
26. *Frankfurter Allgemeine Zeitung*, 8 May 1992.
27. *Frankfurter Allgemeine Zeitung*, 13 April 1994.
28. In 1969 it came in fact very close to the five per cent border, but certainly during the 1969 election campaign the party did not expect to be so close to exclusion from the Bundestag. In 1983, though starting the election campaign from a low base of opinion poll support, there were clear signs of improvement throughout the campaign, and both the 'Genscher factor' and support because of its role in bringing about the change of government in 1982 were (correctly, as it happened) expected to help the party. On split-voting campaigns of the FDP, see Geoffrey K. Roberts, '"The Second-Vote" Strategy of the West German Free Democratic Party', *European Journal of Political Research*, vol.16, no.3 (1988), pp.317–37.
29. Patrick Moreau, 'Die PDS: eine post-kommunistische Partei'. *Aus Politik und Zeitgeschichte*, 5, 24 Jan. 1992, pp.35–44. See also Emil-Peter Müller, 'Quo vadis, PDS?', *Politische Studien*, no.318 (July -August 1991), p.397, which foresaw the PDS at best surviving at the level of Länder politics in east Germany. Ute Schmidt, in 'Die Parteienlandschaft in Deutschland nach der Vereinigung', *Gegenwartskunde*, vol.40 no.4 (1991), p.536, predicted that the PDS would find its electoral support melting away, if the SPD produced policies appropriate to the needs of east Germany.
30. Ilse Spittmann, 'PDS – Anwalt der Ostdeutschen?', *Deutschland Archiv*, July 1994, p.673; Jürgen P. Land and Patrick Moreau, 'PDS: Das Erbe der Diktatur', *Politische Studien*, Sept. 1994, p.9.
31. In a survey 76 per cent of west Germans, but only 13 per cent of east Germans, and only 6 per cent of PDS supporters believed that democracy was the best form of state. 75 per cent of PDS supporters, 51 per cent of east Germans, but only 3 per cent of west Germans placed equality ahead of freedom as a value (Elisabeth Noelle-Neumann. 'Wenig Neigung zur Demokratie', *Frankfurter Allgemeine Zeitung*, 28 June 1994).
32. Geoffrey K. Roberts, '"Emigrants in their own Country": German Reunification and its Political Consequences', *Parliamentary Affairs*, July 1991, pp.386–7.
33. On the creation of the *Gerechtigkeitkomitees* (Committees for Justice), see *Der Spiegel*, 15 June 1992, p.17; *Das Parlament*, 26 June 1992.
34. *Frankfurter Allgemeine Zeitung*, 25 March 1994. 71 per cent of east German respondents in a survey agreed that they wanted the PDS to return to the Bundestag in 1994: Heinrich Bortfeldt, 'Auf dass der Wind sich drehe!', *Deutschland Archiv*, April 1994, p.340.
35. Moreau and Neu, op. cit. p.9; Spittmann, 'PDS – Anwalt der Ostdeutschen?', p.673.
36. *Frankfurter Allgemeine Zeitung*, 29 July 1994.
37. *Das Parlament*, 3 May and 14/21 June 1991; *Frankfurter Allgemeine Zeitung*, 29 April and 13 May 1991.
38. *Frankfurter Allgemeine Zeitung*, 14 May 1991.

39. Other factors affect the relationship between the Greens and the PDS. For example, the academic-intelligentsia constituency which provides Greens votes in west Germany tends to vote PDS in east Germany (*Der Spiegel*, 19 Sept. 1994, p.26). Tactically, by forcing the PDS in Sachsen-Anhalt to abandon their position of total opposition, the Greens (and SPD) could claim that they were putting the PDS on the horns of a dilemma (*Frankfurter Allgemeine Zeitung*, 9 July 1994).

40. *Frankfurter Allgemeine Zeitung*, 12 March 1994.

41. Hubert Kleinert, *Vom Protest- zur Regierungspartei. Die Geschichte der Grünen*, (Frankfurt am Main, Eichborn Verlag, 1992) p.11.

42. *Frankfurter Allgemeine Zeitung*, 22 Jan. 1994; *Der Spiegel*, 3 Oct. 1994, p.24; *Suddeutsche Zeitung*, 4 Oct. 1994; *Das Parlament*, 7 Oct. 1994.

43. *Frankfurter Allgemeine Zeitung*, 28 Feb. 1994.

44. Thomas Poguntke and Rüdiger Schmitt-Back, 'Still the same with a new name? Bündis '90/Die Grünen after the fusion', *German Politics*, 1994 p.98. Poguntke and Schmitt-Beck note (op. cit., p.96) that at the time of the merger the Greens had 37,891 members (but only 1,246 in east Germany: 3.3 per cent), whereas Alliance '90 had 2,709 members; only 123 of which were in west Germany. Alliance '90 thus contributed 6.6 per cent of the total membership, and even in east Germany constituted only two-thirds of the membership of the new party.

45. *Frankfurter Allgemeine Zeitung*, 9 June 1994.

46. Carl Christian Kaiser, 'Es rumort im Bürgertum', *Die Zeit*, 26 Nov. 1993.

47. Some CDU members in Hamburg had taken the party to court because, they claimed, its candidate-selection procedures were unconstitutional. The court upheld this complaint in a decision in May 1993, forcing the re-run of the Land election originally held in June 1991. An initiative by some of those dissident CDU members led to the formation of the STATT-party on 30 June 1993.

48. Peter Gluchowski and Jürgen Hoffmann, *STATT Partei: Aufstieg und schneller Fall einer Protestpartei* (Sankt Augustin, Konrad-Adenauer Stiftung: Interne Studien 81/1994), p.43; Forschungsgruppe Wahlen, *Wahl in Hamburg*, (Mannheim, Forschugsgruppe Wahlen, 1993), p.25.

49. Thomas Kleine-Brockhoff and Dirk Kurbjuweit, 'Die Bürger-Wehr', *Die Zeit*, 21 Jan. 1994. This article also refers to local successes of new parties in Bremen and Rüsselsheim. See also the editorial: 'Verlorene Liebesmüh', *Frankfurter Allgemeine Zeitung*, 9 June 1994.

50. *Der Spiegel*, 29 Aug. 1994, p.16. Schönhuber was expelled from his post as chairman by his party Executive committee, but fought this. However, this merely delayed the change of leader (*Suddeutsche Zeitung*, 4 Oct. 1994; *Der Spiegel*, 10 Oct. 1994, p.25 and 26 Dec. 1994, p.35).

51. *Der Spiegel*, 21 Nov. 1994, p.61.

52. Claus Leggewie: 'Aus Anti-Effekten Zustimmung mobilisieren', *Frankfurter Allgemeine Zeitung*, 19 April 1993.

53. *Der Spiegel*, 26 Dec. 1994, p.29.

54. *Der Spiegel*, 28 Nov. 1994, pp.21–2.

Election Trends in Germany.
An Analysis of the Second General Election
in Reunited Germany

WOLFGANG G. GIBOWSKI

As in previous Bundestag elections, issues, images of leading candidates and of the parties themselves, and the degree of voter loyalty all contributed in 1994 to an explanation of the Bundestag election outcome. Changes in the voter profile for the parties in terms of gender, age and social composition were also significant factors. The 1994 election has important implications for the future development of the party system.

The results of the second general election to be held in reunited Germany confirmed once again the experience accumulated over the years in western Germany that incumbent federal governments do not normally lose elections. In the history of the Federal Republic of Germany no opposition has ever succeeded in ousting an incumbent government on the basis of a general election. The change of government that took place in connection with the 1969 general election was exclusively the result of a change in coalition structures.

Two requirements have always been involved in the analysis of past general elections: an analysis of the factors that have brought about the kind of consistency in individual voting patterns that has been observed to date in a large proportion of the electorate in the western part of the country and an explanation as to what current political influences any changes in voting patterns can be attributed to. The reunification of Germany has made it necessary to apply the kind of election analysis typical of the western part of the country to western and eastern Germany separately. Answering the question as to who voted for whom, that is analysing voting patterns in the various relevant groups in Germany society, also requires a separate analysis of the old and the new Länder. In this context it is necessary to ask the question as to whether the stable voting behaviour observed in certain socio-structural groups of western Germany has a counterpart in eastern Germany.

1. The Political Issues Presented by the Parties, the Role Played by Leading Candidates and Tactical Voting

The first point of analysis involves the factors underlying voter volatility. At the individual level this means distinguishing voters with a stable sense of party loyalty from those whose party preferences are potentially open. The way the latter group of voters cast their ballot is the consequence of a number of overlapping and interlinked factors. It is among these voters that the parties have the greatest chance of bringing about a change in political preferences. The 'Michigan school' sees the opportunities for parties to win votes in three areas:[1] in the perception of leading politicians; in the perception of a party image; and in the perceived ability of leading candidates and their parties to solve major problems. The way these factors are perceived is of decisive importance in determining what party a swing voter will cast his ballot for. The way in which a leading candidate is accepted by his party and how convincingly the parties and leading candidates can present[2] their views on major issues are of key importance in this context.

With the exception of 1957, all the general elections held in the Federal Republic of Germany both before and after reunification have led to coalition governments. The reasons for this lie in a combination of political interest groups and the established system of proportional representation. Almost of necessity, the coalition planning and tactical voting behaviour found in Germany forms an important addition to the model developed by the 'Michigan school'. In connection with tactical voting trends the three areas of influence already mentioned are complemented by considerations as to how a specific government coalition can be achieved. In the case of the 1994 general election the two coalition alternatives were the CDU–CSU and FDP, on the one hand, and the SPD and the Greens, on the other. Voters who identify with one of these two coalition alternatives can vote for either of the parties in the respective coalition camps with a view to optimising the effect of their vote. Needless to say, polls assessing the chances of parties play a very important role in this connection.

Current factors determining voter decisions need to be viewed as a single complex of factors in which particular importance attaches to personal elements. In this age of communications there is a need to present political issues to the electorate. However, addressing major issues from the standpoint of the parties and their leading candidates will have a limited effect if it is done by a politician who is not very popular and therefore is not listened to. A genuinely popular candidate, on the other hand, can, at least for a certain amount of time, compensate for image problems regarding perceived competence and other deficits the party in question may have.

FIGURE 1
THE MOST IMPORTANT ISSUES

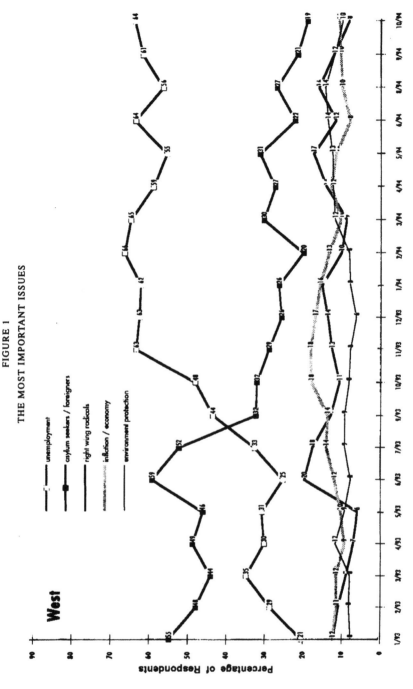

Source: Monthly Polls of the Forschungsgruppe Wahlen e.V. Mannheim; Graphics: BPA

FIGURE 2
THE MOST IMPORTANT ISSUES

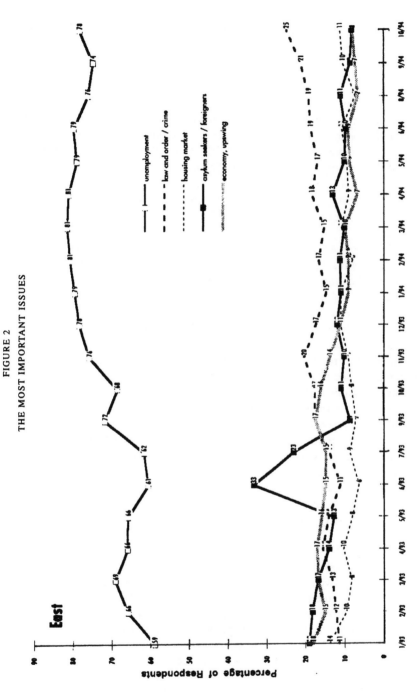

Source: Monthly Polls of the Forschungsgruppe Wahlen e.V. Mannheim; Graphics: BPA

Past experience has shown that the popularity of a leading politician does not automatically translate into votes. If a politician has good approval ratings and if the polls show that a majority of those interviewed might even like to see this person be chancellor, this does not automatically mean that the people in question would vote for his party. This was documented very clearly in connection with the 1980 general election when more than 60 per cent of those polled said they would like to see the incumbent chancellor, the SPD's leading candidate, Helmut Schmidt, as chancellor and only 29 per cent expressed support for Franz-Josef Strauss, the leading candidate of the CSU. However, in the general election held shortly thereafter the CDU–CSU received 44.5 per cent of the votes cast and the SPD only 42.9 per cent.[3]

Why, then, are leading politicians so important for their parties? The main factors for changes in voting behaviour are intertwined in a complex manner. The importance of an individual factor cannot be determined precisely. Leading politicians have a very special responsibility in connection with explaining relatively abstract party policy issues to the electorate. Given contradictory views on the part of experts, many fiercely debated political issues cannot be decided on rationally by voters and, as such, become matters of belief. The more sophisticated political issues become and the more difficult it becomes for voters to understand foreign policy, economic and military decisions, the more individual voters need to rely on the expertise of their political representatives. As a rule, the popularity of a politician reflects how much competence the voters attribute to him. This is where the connection between politicians and their parties becomes evident. A popular politician will have fewer problems explaining his position on political issues than one who is less popular. Thus, the popularity of leading politicians is valuable not so much in its ability to attract votes to a given party as in the ability of these candidates to convey controversial party political issues to the electorate.

Major Issues in Election Year 1994

The past few years in western and eastern Germany have been rich in issues and problems. Two issues were of particular importance in the west: worries about unemployment and concern about the influx of asylum seekers and foreigners, a matter that for some time appeared to be out of control. This issue, in particular, had strongly preoccupied German politics for many years and generated far-reaching political and social debates. As a result of the constant influx of asylum seekers and foreigners this issue moved to the top of the list of important political issues in September 1991, where it remained until July 1993.[4] The issue only began to lose importance in the eyes of the public when the governing parties and the SPD opposition reached an agreement on amending Germany's asylum laws. This led very rapidly to a decline in the number of asylum seekers. As a consequence, the issue lost importance in the eyes of the western German public. The right-wing Republicans profited from the public debate conducted on the strong influx of asylum seekers and foreigners. The right-wing 'Republikaner' made a comeback parallel to the emergence of this issue and in April 1992 were elected to the Baden-Württemberg Land parliament with 10.9 per cent of the vote. Support for the 'Republikaner' declined parallel to the loss in importance of the asylum-seeker issue. It was for this reason that they failed to be re-elected to the European Parliament. Since autumn 1993 the dominant concern has been unemployment, ending for the most part the differences that had existed up to then between the western and eastern German agendas.

Since reunification the agenda of major issues in the eastern German Länder has been dominated exclusively by worries relating to the high level of unemployment.[5] The asylum-seeker issue, which was so important in western Germany for a long period of time, became prominent in the new Länder only for a short period of time in the summer of 1993. The relatively low level of importance attributed to this issue in the new Länder is a result of the fact that most asylum seekers and ethnic German resettlers prefer to settle in the western Länder. A further issue, environmental protection, which has continued to be the third most important issue in the western part of the country, has been completely insignificant in eastern Germany. The dominant issues in both western and eastern Germany relate to everyday concerns. Bread-and-butter issues dominate, while post-material issues are of peripheral importance in the west and without any importance at all in the east.

Importance of Leading Candidates and Perceived Party Competence

The prospects of the Bonn government, made up of the CDU–CSU and the FDP, winning the general election last Autumn were still being assessed very pessimistically in the spring of 1994. Nearly all the polls reflected a rather critical public mood concerning the federal government and its leading representatives.

This political mood was reflected in perceptions of the two leading candidates, Chancellor Helmut Kohl and his challenger from the SPD, Rudolf Scharping. At the beginning of 1994, 52 per cent of the Germans in the eastern and western parts of the country indicated they would like to see Rudolf Scharping become the next chancellor, as opposed to 34 per cent who wanted to see the incumbent Chancellor, Helmut Kohl, re-elected.

A question regarding significant personality traits of the two candidates for the chancellorship showed that Helmut Kohl was seen by a majority of

FIGURE 3

PUBLIC EXPECTATIONS ABOUT THE ECONOMY AND THE ELECTION WINNER

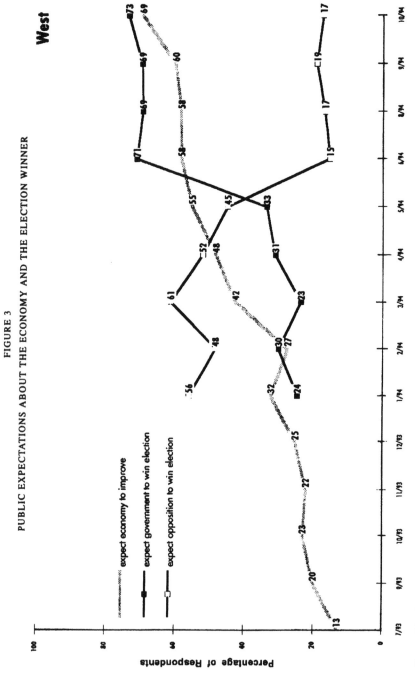

Source: Monthly Polls of the Forschungsgruppe Wahlen e.V. Mannheim; Graphics: BPA

FIGURE 4

PUBLIC EXPECTATIONS ABOUT THE ECONOMY AND THE ELECTION WINNER

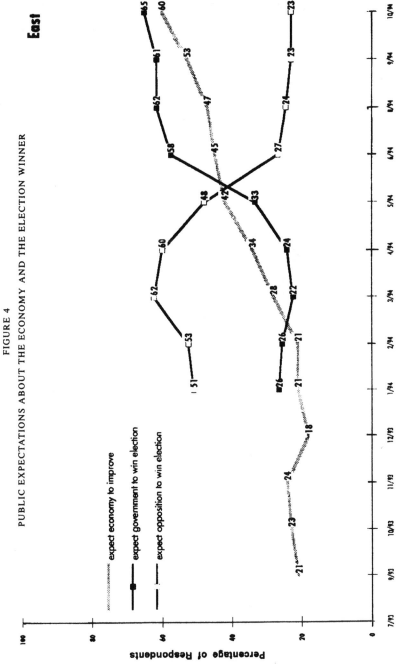

Source: Monthly Polls of the Forschungsgruppe Wahlen e. V. Mannheim; Graphics: BPA

FIGURE 5
PREFERRED CHANCELLOR

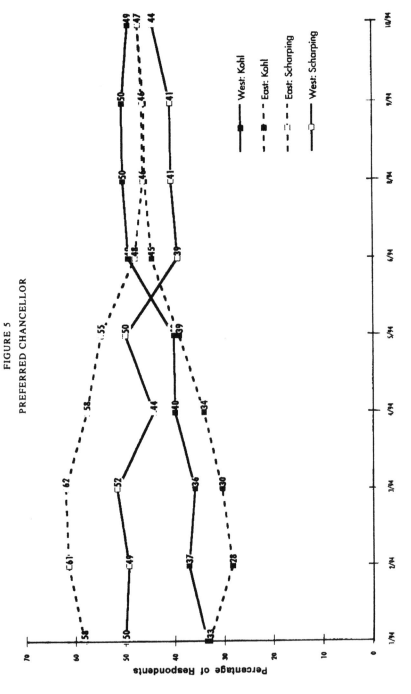

Source: Monthly Polls of the Forschungsgruppe Wahlen e.V. Mannheim; Graphics: BPA

the population as being more energetic, a stronger leader, a man better suited to lead a government and, in particular, superior in representing German interests in dealings with other countries. On the other hand, the majority of those polled at that point in time viewed Scharping as being a more suitable person to resolve Germany's economic problems. Attribution of this ability to Scharping was, however, totally atypical for a leading SPD candidate. Since the founding of the (western German) Federal Republic economic competence has been attributed almost exclusively to the CDU. The first Minister of Economics, Ludwig Erhard, established the CDU's reputation as an 'economic party' with the success of his social market economy system. Scharping's lead over Kohl in this area, a key issue for most Germans, reflected the loss of economic competence suffered by the CDU-led government as of mid-1993. As of the end of that year nearly 40 per cent of those polled in western and eastern Germany felt an SPD-led government would be more competent in resolving the country's economic problems. Only 30 per cent of western Germans and 20 per cent of eastern Germans felt the Bonn coalition had this competence.[6] This loss of competence in economic matters had a negative effect on public perceptions of the governing parties as well as on Helmut Kohl's approval ratings.

It was of far-reaching importance that Chancellor Helmut Kohl was in the vanguard of those who stated their firm belief in economic recovery and that he recurrently pointed out initial signs of improvement in the economic situation. In this way he succeeded more and more in associating himself and his party with the process of economic recovery. Kohl's optimism had initially been dismissed as campaign gesturing, but it soon became evident that his assertions were correct. The economic situation in Germany improved steadily and independent economic research institutes confirmed this with increasing frequency. The results of a poll in which the following question was asked: 'In your view, is the German economy currently on the upswing again or do you feel that this is not the case?' provided very accurate information of public perceptions of the economic situation in the election year. Whereas in February only 27 per cent of western Germans believed the economy was recovering, in March it was 42 per cent, and in May 55 per cent. In the new Länder the results of this poll were similarly positive, although at a somewhat lower level.

In both western and eastern Germany the trend shown by public expectations with regard to economic recovery was in covariance with public expectations that the incumbent Bonn government would win the general election. As of June 1994 the number of people both in western and eastern Germany who doubted that Helmut Kohl's government would win the election had dwindled significantly. The fact that the process of economic recovery occurred exactly as Helmut Kohl had been saying it would since the autumn of 1993 was perceived as a success of the incumbent government, particularly the CDU, and was ultimately what determined the outcome of the election.[7] This factor greatly improved public perceptions with regard to the incumbent government's economic competence. Since April 1994 most of those polled in western Germany again attributed superior economic competence to the incumbent government. This trend was not quite as rapid in eastern Germany. From June onwards the percentage of those polled who attributed more economic competence to the incumbent government or the opposition was about the same.

As the polls showed steadily improving results with regard to economic recovery and growing certainty that the incumbent Bonn government would win the election, more and more voters indicated they would prefer to see Helmut Kohl become the future chancellor.

In May and June 1994[8] Helmut Kohl overtook Rudolf Scharping in the western German opinion polls, whereas in the new Länder they were in a neck-and-neck race right up to election day. From then on Helmut Kohl consistently received better approval ratings in western Germany than his challenger from the SPD. The Chancellor's approval ratings improved significantly both in western and eastern Germany, whereas Scharping's approval ratings declined significantly over the same period of time. Needless to say, the fact that the economic situation improved dramatically in Germany was a key factor in improving the approval ratings of Helmut Kohl, the CDU and the government in general. In May the independent economic research institutes were forecasting GNP growth of 2.5 per cent. Six months earlier their forecast had been 1.5 per cent.

The SPD and Rudolf Scharping attempted to prevent the emerging change of public mood in favour of the incumbent government. In place of other issues the SPD conducted a public debate over a period of several months with the CDU and the CSU on who should succeed Richard von Weizsäcker as president. The debate served as a kind of test of the political climate in Germany. Although the CDU and CSU have far more representatives in the body that elects the federal president than the SPD, the SPD tried to create the impression that the chances of the SPD candidate for the presidency, the very popular premier of Nordrhein-Westfalen, Johannes Rau, were much better than was actually the case. When the CDU–CSU candidate, Roman Herzog, was elected, there was disappointment in the ranks of the SPD. To a certain extent Rudolf Scharping was blamed personally for this. On the basis of the polls taken in the first half of the year it had appeared for some time as if the SPD might be able to overtake the CDU–CSU in the fourth European Parliament election, held in mid-June. The SPD had only managed to do this in a national election once in the past, by a narrow margin in the 1972 general election. However, things were to turn out differently. The CDU–CSU gained additional votes in the European election, while the SPD sustained significant losses. Although the result of the European election cannot be assessed as an indicator for the general election, given the traditional low voter turnout in European elections, it did change the political climate in favour of the CDU–CSU. At the same time, the result of the European election documented the weakness of the FDP, a trend that had already been reflected in the polls. The FDP failed to get over the (countrywide) five per cent hurdle both in western and eastern Germany. In addition to the good results attained by the Greens, a confirmation of the results they were getting in the opinion polls, the fact that the radical right-wing 'Republikaner' lost significantly and did not make it over the five per cent hurdle was a significant development. The fact that the PDS received nearly 20 per cent of the vote in the new Länder (as opposed to 4.7 per cent countrywide) also attracted considerable attention. It showed that despite the emerging process of economic recovery, also perceived as such in eastern Germany, there continued to be significant potential for public dissatisfaction.[9]

The Land parliament election held in Sachsen-Anhalt shortly after the European Parliament election also influenced the political mood in Germany, but from an entirely different perspective. To the surprise of many observers, the CDU again received a majority of votes, despite massive losses. However, since the FDP failed to get over the five per cent hurdle it was not possible to continue the CDU–FDP coalition. Instead of forming a grand coalition with the CDU, the SPD chose to form a minority government with Alliance 90/The Greens, which for all practical intents and purposes made them dependent on the votes of the PDS. The CDU protested sharply against the formation of a government in which it was not involved. In this connection the CDU initiated its 'red socks' campaign, attracting a great deal of public attention to the two major parties.

After the summer recess Land parliament elections were held in Brandenburg, Sachsen and Bayern. Although the nature of Land parliament elections is considerably different from that of general elections, they were seen as a test of the public mood prior to the general election. Since the FDP failed to take the five per cent hurdle in all three of these elections, the possibility that the FDP might also not succeed in the general election became an increasingly frequent subject of discussion. This made voters interested in seeing a continuation of the CDU–CSU and FDP government aware of the need to vote tactically, that is in a manner that would preserve the coalition. The polls made it increasingly clear to tactical voters that Helmut Kohl and the CDU–CSU would only be able to form a government again if the FDP made it into the Bundestag. In the week prior to the general election 65 per cent of those polled in western Germany who intended to vote for the FDP actually preferred the CDU or CSU. In eastern Germany this was the case with 45 per cent of the FDP voters polled.[10]

Although the nature of Land parliament elections is different from that of general elections, the results of the elections in Brandenburg, Sachsen and Bayern reflected the outcome of the general election in rough outline. The fact that the CDU and CSU were able to obtain good results in Sachsen and Bayern while the SPD did very well in Brandenburg showed that the political climate was not one-sidedly in favour of a given party. It also became clearly evident that the Greens are much weaker in eastern Germany than they are in western Germany and that the PDS was clearly in the process of becoming the third-strongest party in eastern Germany.

At this point in time it also became clear that a majority of the electorate did not want a change of government. The hope expressed by the SPD at the beginning of 1994, when the polls showed that 60 per cent of the electorate wanted a change of government,[11] was not long lived. The decline in desire for a change of government shown by the opinion polls indicated that the original wish to have the Bonn government replaced could be explained on the basis of a current critical attitude with regard to the governing parties and less on the basis of a definitive wish to have this government replaced at all costs.

2. Voter Trends in Terms of Demographic and Social Structures

From the standpoint of electoral sociology the results achieved by the parties within various groups in society in which traditional loyalties exist with regard to the major parties is of particular interest in western Germany.[12] With regard to the new Länder the question immediately arises as to the extent to which the patterns that apply to western Germany are also valid in eastern Germany and to what extent stability and change can be observed in comparison with the first general election. The extremely strong fluctuations, that is from a western German viewpoint, in the opinion polls conducted in the new Länder in the course of the past few years seem to point to a high level of voter volatility in eastern Germany. While the voter trends in the various religious and professional groups are of particular interest from the standpoint of electoral sociology, voter trends in the various age and gender categories are of even greater interest from a political standpoint. The underrepresentation of a party in a given age or gender group usually leads directly to the conclusion that there is a specific issue-related deficit in the interest sphere of the group of persons in question.

Voter Trends Based on Age and Gender

The CDU and CSU tend to do particularly well among older voters, whereas the SPD tends to attract the support of younger voters. In the case of the SPD, however, the differences between the age groups are not nearly as great as in the case of the CDU and CSU. The Greens have a very distinctive age profile. Half of their voters are under the age of 34.

The differences in male and female voter trends tend to be slight. The CDU–CSU and the Greens are more successful with women than with men. More men than women vote for the FDP. The SPD and the PDS have almost equal numbers of male and female voters (Tables 1 and 2).

The differences in voting trends become greater if we combine the age and gender factors. In this case the CDU–CSU does significantly worse among young women than among young men both in western and eastern Germany. The very young voter profile the SPD had in the past has been lost as a result of the Greens. In the new Länder (Table 2) strong changes can be seen in the case of the SPD, the FDP and the PDS. The CDU sustained significant losses among older male voters, a relatively poor result in an age group that is otherwise a strong source of support. In the eastern Länder the SPD made considerable gains in the middle age groups. The PDS made its strongest gains among younger voters, particularly among women.

Voting Trends in Social Groups

Over a period of decades it has been observed in western Germany that preferences for the CDU–CSU or SPD exist in certain groups in German society and that these preferences are not affected by current political events, leading candidates and public debate on key issues. The reasons for this lie in political conflict structures (cleavages) that are reflected in the system of political parties.[13] In the case of the SPD there are strong ties to the labour movement which go back to the times of the Industrial Revolution. In the case of the CDU–CSU there are strong ties to the Catholic population, whose loyalty was originally to the old Zentrum party. When the western German Federal Republic was founded the Catholics accepted the CDU as the successor party to the Zentrum. In these two groups – the labour movement and Catholics – the majority of voters support the SPD or the CDU–CSU respectively. Although these groups are diminishing in size as a result of processes of modernisation in society, their respective party loyalties are still clearly evident and guarantee the CDU–CSU as well as the SPD a reliable, but slowly and constantly declining, voter base.

In western Germany there have been significant changes in social structures relating to membership in religious groups and to membership in

TABLE 1
PARTY SUPPORT BY GENDER AND AGE. RESULTS 1994 AND DIFFERENCES TO 1990 IN WEST GERMANY

TOTAL

Age group	CDU/CSU	Difference 1990	SPD	Difference 1990	FDP	Difference 1990	Grüne	Difference 1990
18-24	34,2	-1,9	36,3	-0,8	6,8	-3,4	14,9	+5,1
25-34	32,3	-1,9	41,1	-0,7	5,7	-3,4	14,1	+4,3
35-44	36,4	-3,1	39,3	+1,0	7,2	-4,7	12,2	+6,1
45-59	45,6	-2,0	37,5	+3,1	8,6	-3,2	4,5	+2,6
60 and older	50,7	-2,4	34,9	+1,7	8,5	0,0	2,5	+1,8
Total	42,1	-2,2	37,5	+1,8	7,7	-2,9	7,9	+3,1

MEN

Age group	CDU/CSU	Difference 1990	SPD	Difference 1990	FDP	Difference 1990	Grüne	Difference 1990
18-24	36,2	-1,0	34,4	-1,1	7,1	-3,3	13,4	+4,6
25-34	34,8	+0,2	38,0	-2,8	6,1	-3,3	13,1	+4,0
35-44	35,2	-3,5	40,8	+2,6	7,6	-4,2	10,7	+4,6
45-59	44,8	-1,8	37,3	+2,4	9,6	-2,3	4,2	+2,5
60 and older	50,4	+0,2	34,3	+0,3	9,7	+0,8	1,9	+1,2
Total	41,4	-1,2	37,0	0,5	8,3	-2,3	7,7	3,1

WOMEN

Age group	CDU/CSU	Difference 1990	SPD	Difference 1990	FDP	Difference 1990	Grüne	Difference 1990
18-24	31,9	-3,1	37,8	-1,2	6,8	-3,1	16,8	+5,9
25-34	29,5	-4,2	44,5	+1,7	5,3	-3,5	15,5	+5,0
35-44	37,4	-2,8	37,4	-1,0	7,0	-5,0	14,0	+7,9
45-59	47,1	-1,6	36,6	+2,6	8,0	-3,7	5,1	+3,0
60 and older	52,9	-2,1	32,8	+0,2	8,1	-0,2	3,2	+2,5
Total	42,8	-2,5	37,0	+0,8	7,3	-2,7	8,9	+4,3

Source: Exit Polls of the Forschungsgruppe Wahlen 1994 and Respresentative Electoral Statistics 1990

TABLE 2

PARTY SUPPORT BY GENDER AND AGE. RESULTS 1994 AND DIFFERENCES TO 1990 IN EAST GERMANY

TOTAL

Age group	CDU	Difference 1990	SPD	Difference 1990	FDP	Difference 1990	Grüne	Difference 1990	PDS	Difference 1990
18-24	29,2	-3,8	25,8	+3,5	3,7	-8,1	10,4	-1,8	22,6	+11,1
25-34	31,2	-5,6	32,3	+8,2	3,4	-8,7	6,4	-2,7	23,0	+11,2
35-44	37,7	-2,5	31,6	+9,8	4,2	-10,8	3,9	-2,8	21,4	+9,8
45-59	39,5	-3,3	32,8	+8,7	3,9	-10,7	3,3	-0,8	19,0	+7,7
60 and older	45,2	-1,4	31,5	+5,2	2,9	-8,0	2,3	+0,7	16,9	+5,2
Total	38,5	-3,3	31,5	+7,2	3,5	-9,4	4,3	-1,9	19,8	+8,7

MEN

Age group	CDU	Difference 1990	SPD	Difference 1990	FDP	Difference 1990	Grüne	Difference 1990	PDS	Difference 1990
18-24	30,0	-3,0	23,0	+2,0	4,4	-7,0	10,2	-0,6	21,7	+10,1
25-34	35,6	-1,8	31,4	+7,8	3,9	-7,8	4,4	-3,8	18,8	+7,3
35-44	37,2	-2,7	32,9	+10,8	4,4	-10,1	4,3	-1,6	19,9	+8,0
45-59	41,2	+0,2	31,9	+6,6	4,6	-10,1	2,4	-1,0	18,7	+6,8
60 and older	35,2	-6,2	36,1	+7,4	2,3	-8,7	1,4	-0,2	23,1	+8,8
Total	36,9	-2,5	31,8	+7,1	3,9	-9,1	3,8	-1,4	20,3	+8,0

WOMEN

Age group	CDU	Difference 1990	SPD	Difference 1990	FDP	Difference 1990	Grüne	Difference 1990	PDS	Difference 1990
18-24	25,2	-7,7	29,9	+6,2	3,0	-9,2	10,9	-2,7	25,0	+13,6
25-34	27,5	-8,7	33,7	+9,1	2,9	-9,7	8,6	-1,4	26,0	+14,0
35-44	37,9	-2,5	30,3	+8,8	4,0	-11,5	3,9	-3,5	22,6	+11,3
45-59	37,5	-6,9	32,5	+9,7	3,7	-10,7	4,4	-0,3	20,4	+9,8
60 and older	50,9	+1,2	29,3	+4,4	3,1	-7,7	3,2	+1,6	12,6	+2,4
Total	39,1	-4,0	31,0	+7,4	3,4	-9,6	5,2	-0,6	19,7	+8,8

Source: Exit Polls of the Forschungsgruppe Wahlen 1994 and Respresentative Electoral Statistics 1990

the various occupational groups (see Tables 3 and 4). Reunification has resulted in the two major religious groups being approximately the same size throughout Germany, while the group of those without a religion or of a different religious denomination now amounts to nearly 30 per cent of the population.

Reunification has reduced the number of self-employed persons and increased the number of blue-collar workers.

TABLE 3

RELIGIOUS AFFILIATION

Religion	Protestants	Catholics	others/none
Germany	35,7	34,7	29,6
West Germany	38,1	42,9	19,0
East Germany	27,0	5,9	67,0

Percentage of the Population (Germans and Foreigners), 31.12.1992

Source: Statistical Yearbook of Germany 1994

TABLE 4

EMPLOYED PERSONS

	Self Employed	Civil Servants	White Collor Workers	Blue Collor Workers
Germany	8,4	6,7	45,6	37,8
West Germany without Berlin	9,0	7,9	44,7	36,7
East Germany incl. Berlin	5,7	1,6	49,8	42,7

Percentage of Employed Persons, May 1994

Source: Statistical Yearbook of Germany 1994

Voting Trends and Religion

Voting trends in the various religious groups confirmed past observations for western Germany as well as for the new Länder in eastern Germany. The CDU–CSU attracts more voter support among Catholics in western Germany and the few Catholics who live in eastern Germany than among Protestants. Conversely, the SPD attracts more voter support among Protestants than among Catholics, both in western and eastern Germany. In western Germany the SPD also attracts more voter support among persons without religious affiliations. As was seen in the 1990 election, being a member of the Protestant faith has different implications in eastern Germany than it does in western Germany.[14] Most of those who preserved their religious affiliations under the eastern Germany communist regime were in opposition to the regime. Today they see their values represented more by the CDU than by any other party. This also explains why, in comparison with the 1990 general election, there were greater differences for the CDU–CSU in western Germany than in eastern Germany, where the CDU sustained heavy losses only among those voters without religious affiliations. The SPD, on the other hand, made strong gains among both Catholics and Protestants in eastern Germany, a trend doubtless favoured by the losses suffered by the FDP and the Greens in these groups. The gains made by the PDS were primarily in the group of voters without religious affiliations.

The level of voter loyalty towards the CDU–CSU is particularly high among Catholics with strong church ties. The CDU–CSU did not do quite as well among Catholics with strong church ties as it did in 1990; however, the result attained is comparable with past general elections (information on church ties is not available for eastern Germany).

In general it can be said that a cleavage based on religion continues to exist in western Germany. In eastern Germany a cleavage of this kind does not exist between Catholics and Protestants, but rather between voters with religious ties and those without. It can be said that the factor 'religion' exerted a stabilising influence on the election results achieved by the CDU–CSU in the 1994 general election.

Voting Trends, Occupation and Union Membership

The SPD made gains among blue-collar workers both in western and eastern Germany. However, despite strong losses, the CDU still attracted more blue-collar votes in eastern Germany than the SPD.[15] The 1994 general election brought significant improvement for the SPD in this social group, to which it attributes particular importance.

Traditional blue-collar loyalty to the SPD is stronger when the voters in question are also members of a union (comparable information is not available for eastern Germany).

In the traditional core group of loyal SPD voters, that is blue-collar union members, the SPD was able to recoup the losses suffered in the 1990 general election, although this result was still not comparable with the level of blue-collar voter support received in earlier elections. The CDU, on the other hand, registered significant losses among blue-collar workers, independent of their union membership. The considerable changes in voter trends noted in the various occupational groups with and without union affiliations benefited the SPD in particular. In eastern Germany a trend towards western structures seems to be taking place.

TABLE 5

PARTY SUPPORT BY RELIGION. RESULTS 1994 AND DIFFRENCES TO 1990

WEST GERMANY

Religion	CDU/CSU	Difference 1990	SPD	Difference 1990	FDP	Difference 1990	Grüne	Difference 1990	PDS	Difference 1990
Catholics	51,6	-4,7	30,6	-4,0	6,8	-2,0	6,3	+1,8	0,6	+0,5
Protestants	36,5	-3,1	43,7	+4,0	8,2	-5,1	7,8	+3,5	0,7	+0,5
unaffiliated	28,0	+2,3	40,1	+4,9	8,3	-3,1	14,9	+3,2	3,2	+1,8

EAST GERMANY

Religion	CDU	Difference 1990	SPD	Difference 1990	FDP	Difference 1990	Grüne	Difference 1990	PDS	Difference 1990
Catholics	68,5	+2,7	19,5	+8,0	2,5	-8,9	2,5	-3,8	2,9	+1,4
Protestants	53,4	0,0	28,9	+8,8	4,7	-10,7	5,0	-1,1	6,3	+4,5
unaffiliated	27,1	-6,2	34,1	+5,4	3,1	-9,8	4,3	-4,5	28,8	+15,9

Source: Exit Polls of the Forschungsgruppe Wahlen 1994 and 1990

TABLE 6
PARTY SUPPORT AND CHURCH ATTENDANCE IN WEST GERMANY (IN PER CENT)

Catholics

	often						sometimes						never					
	1976	1980	1983	1987	1990	1994	1976	1980	1983	1987	1990	1994	1976	1980	1983	1987	1990	1994
CDU/CSU	82	74	78	70	78	74	58	54	65	53	59	54	36	36	50	40	34	37
FDP	2	7	3	6	5	6	9	10	8	7	9	8	3	5	4	7	10	7
SPD	16	19	16	19	9	14	32	36	26	35	25	29	60	56	33	40	37	41
GRÜNE	-	0	3	4	4	2	-	0	1	4	4	6	-	3	13	10	8	9
N =	239	171	152	306	125	1440	149	128	110	255	162	1772	142	141	143	257	101	2591

Non-catholics

	often						sometimes						never					
	1976	1980	1983	1987	1990	1994	1976	1980	1983	1987	1990	1994	1976	1980	1983	1987	1990	1994
CDU/CSU	60	43	54	51	65	47	45	40	48	35	40	42	30	27	35	31	31	32
FDP	11	18	10	12	13	9	10	19	3	13	15	10	10	15	4	9	12	8
SPD	30	36	36	27	11	30	45	41	45	47	37	40	60	56	54	47	44	47
GRÜNE	-	4	0	9	2	8	-	0	4	5	3	5	-	2	7	12	8	9
N =	41	40	52	67	36	366	168	129	134	241	238	1864	297	305	292	502	186	3509

Source: 1976–1990: Forschungsgruppe Wahlen e.V., Gesamtdeutsche Bestätigung für die Bonner Regierungskoalition, a.a.O., S. 647 1994: Exit Polls of the Forschungsgruppe Wahlen

TABLE 7
PARTY SUPPORT BY PROFESSION. RESULTS 1994 AND DIFFERENCES TO 1990 IN GERMANY

WEST GERMANY

Profession	CDU/CSU	Difference 1990	SPD	Difference 1990	FDP	Difference 1990	Grüne	Difference 1990	PDS	Difference 1990
Blue Collar Workers	35,0	-4,0	49,5	+2,8	3,6	-2,4	5,2	+2,0	1,1	+0,9
White Collar Workers	39,9	-3,1	37,7	+1,8	8,4	-3,7	9,6	+4,3	1,0	+0,7
Civil Servants	43,8	*	33,1	*	8,4	*	11,3	*	0,7	*
Farmers	65,4	*	11,9	*	10,6	*	3,6	*	0,9	*
Self Employed	53,0	-3,9	17,1	+0,8	15,7	-2,4	8,4	+3,6	1,4	+1,0

EAST GERMANY

Profession	CDU	Difference 1990	SPD	Difference 1990	FDP	Difference 1990	Grüne	Difference 1990	PDS	Difference 1990
Blue Collar Workers	40,6	-7,9	35,1	+10,4	3,3	-7,1	3,3	-0,8	14,7	+7,4
White Collar Workers	32,0	-3,9	30,7	+5,7	3,9	-10,3	5,3	-3,1	26,3	+12,7
Civil Servants	29,9	*	24,4	*	1,2	*	5,0	*	34,6	*
Farmers	59,0	*	22,2	*	1,5	*	6,5	*	9,8	*
Self Employed	48,3	-0,5	19,7	+3,6	9,7	-10,7	2,4	-1,4	16,9	+11,9

* not asked in 1990

Source: Exit Polls of the Forschungsgruppe Wahlen 1990 and 1994

TABLE 8

PARTY SUPPORT, PROFESSION AND TRADE UNION MEMBERSHIP IN WEST GERMANY (IN PER CENT)

All Respondents

	Members						Non-members					
	1976	1980	1983	1987	1990	1994	1976	1980	1983	1987	1990	1994
CDU/CSU	35	29	36	32	33	32	55	48	56	48	51	45
FDP	9	10	3	3	9	3	8	13	5	11	15	10
SPD	56	58	56	55	49	52	36	38	31	31	28	31
GRÜNE	-	3	5	9	7	7	-	1	7	9	5	9
N =	392	271	278	501	272	1843	700	675	639	1204	664	4316

Blue Collar Workers

	Members						Non-members					
	1976	1980	1983	1987	1990	1994	1976	1980	1983	1987	1990	1994
CDU/CSU	35	29	34	29	37	29	48	36	51	40	49	41
FDP	6	8	3	1	5	1	5	11	2	5	4	4
SPD	58	62	64	60	52	58	47	53	42	47	39	42
GRÜNE	-	1	0	9	4	5	-	0	5	6	6	5
N =	204	153	163	300	95	933	241	181	205	358	128	1138

White Collar Workers and Civil Servants

	Members						Non-members					
	1976	1980	1983	1987	1990	1994	1976	1980	1983	1987	1990	1994
CDU/CSU	35	29	41	36	31	30	55	47	61	50	47	45
FDP	12	14	4	5	11	6	10	13	4	12	19	11
SPD	52	55	48	51	47	50	34	37	26	26	27	31
GRÜNE	-	2	7	7	8	9	-	3	9	10	4	9
N =	161	100	99	168	158	462	282	312	264	550	374	1577

Source: 1976–1990: Forschungsgruppe Wahlen e.V., Gesamtdeutsche Bestätigung für die Bonner Regierungskoalition, a.a.O., S. 645 1994: Exit Polls of the Forschungsgruppe Wahlen

3. Future Prospects

The outcome of the 1994 general election was that the same parties remained in the German Bundestag who were there after the last general election. The FDP and the Greens changed places as the third and fourth strongest parties. The PDS is more strongly represented than it was in 1990. However, questions regarding future prospects for the German system of political parties remain open, since of the five parties represented in the Bundestag, only the CDU–CSU, the SPD and, in part, the Greens appear to be stabilised on the basis of the election results.

Despite the critical situation it was in a year before the general election, the CDU–CSU emerged from the election as the strongest party. If we take into account the challenges this party faced in the first legislative term after reunification and the extent to which social change has undermined the party's sociostructural base, then an election result of well above 40 per cent can be considered a success. It needs to be taken into account here that many CDU and CSU voters cast their second vote for the FDP in order to ensure the survival of the coalition.

The SPD made clear gains over the results it attained in the 1990 general election. As a result of its gains in eastern Germany it has now stabilised as the second strongest party in eastern Germany as well. The SPD made strong gains, particularly in those social groups in which better results had been expected in 1990.

Both in western and eastern Germany the Greens have replaced the FDP as the third strongest party in general elections, but would seem to be stabilised in this sense only in western Germany. Although there are no separate five per cent hurdles for western and eastern Germany, the Greens were unsuccessful in the new Länder. This applies particularly in view of the results the party attained in the Länder parliamentary elections held simultaneously in Thüringen and Mecklenburg-Vorpommern. The Greens had already been unsuccessful in the state parliament elections in Brandenburg and Sachsen. Alliance 90/The Greens, their full party designation, is actually a combination of two completely different parties. In the former GDR the supporters of Alliance 90 do not have the strong environmental orientation of the western German Greens. In 1989 and 1990 they were the advocates of democratic new beginnings. In general, environmental protection does not elicit as much interest in eastern Germany as it does in western Germany, since material needs are still a prominent issue in eastern Germany. It can also be assumed that the debate initiated in Sachsen-Anhalt by the minority government composed of the SPD and Alliance 90/The Greens concerning co-operation with the PDS damaged Alliance 90/The Greens. At any rate, the party was not successful

FIGURE 6

NATIONAL ELECTION 1994 (% Second Ballot)

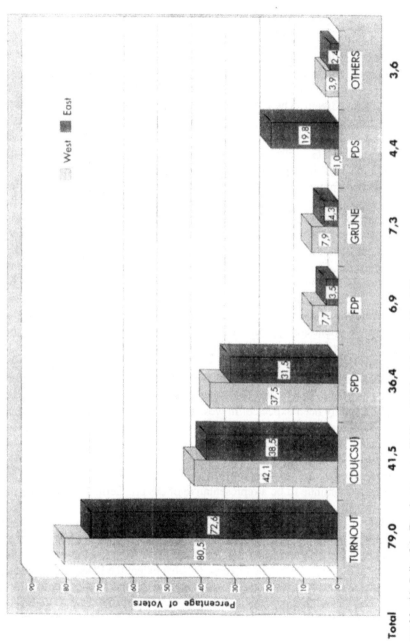

	TURNOUT	CDU(CSU)	SPD	FDP	GRÜNE	PDS	OTHERS
Total	79,0	41,5	36,4	6,9	7,3	4,4	3,6

Source: Monthly Polls of the Forschungsgruppe Wahlen e.V. Mannheim; Graphics: BPA

in any of the four subsequent parliament elections held in the eastern German Länder after the Magdeburg coalition was created. The future of Alliance 90/The Greens in the new Länder will depend on the speed with which the situation in eastern Germany becomes more similar to that in western Germany.

The FDP's situation can certainly be considered less comfortable than that of the Greens. The FDP lost considerable ground in western Germany and dropped to nearly a fourth of its 1990 result in eastern Germany. This is doubtless a direct effect of the very high level of voter volatility there. When Hans-Dietrich Genscher and Otto Graf Lambsdorff retired from the political stage the FDP was left without leaders familiar to the public, a factor of particular importance in eastern Germany. In the short period of time left before the general election Klaus Kinkel was unable to make up for the decades of public exposure these two older politicians had had. In addition, one of the FDP's most important arguments, that it is needed as a necessary element to re-establish the coalition, was not viewed as convincing in the new Länder. There is no tradition and thus no understanding of this type of party function. Prospects for the FDP in eastern Germany, as well as for other parties, will depend on the extent to which it succeeds in finding credible leaders to present issues which the general public perceives as being important and typical for the party in question. Needless to say, this problem also exists in western Germany. However, it is more important in eastern Germany as a result of the level of voter volatility there.

Nothing definitive can be said about the future of the PDS. In eastern Germany the PDS received just under 20 per cent of the vote, far more than had originally been expected. In western Germany it received one per cent. The PDS seeks to attract voter support with two separate images. In eastern Germany the PDS presents itself as a party which addresses the everyday concerns of individual citizens and which can rely on the effective organisational structures established there. Many eastern Germans feel the PDS will continue to be a representative of eastern German interests in the future. In eastern Germany the PDS appeals to those who feel disadvantaged for whatever reason as a result of reunification. In western Germany the PDS presents itself as a genuine left-wing party and is attempting to establish itself as a catch-all party for left-wing voters at the expense of the SPD and the Greens. To what extent the PDS will be able to play a significant role at the national level will depend on the way in which the western German parties, in particular the SPD, respond to the PDS. The PDS is likely to play an important role regionally, that is in the new Länder, for a longer period of time.[16]

If we view the results of the general election separately for western and eastern Germany then what we see is basically two different systems of political parties: the western German four-party system consisting of the CDU–CSU, SPD, FDP and the Greens, on the one hand, and the eastern German three-party system, consisting of the CDU, the SPD and the PDS, on the other. What the future of the countrywide five-party system will be is difficult to forecast, since rising levels of voter volatility have strong implications, particularly with regard to the survival of the smaller parties. Reunification has brought change to the German system of political parties, notwithstanding the stable situation of the CDU–CSU and the SPD, and all indications are that this will continue to be the case for some time to come.

NOTES

I wish to thank Dr Ute Molitor for her help.

Data of Figures: Monthly 1,000 respondents in West Germany and 1,000 respondents in East Germany, each representative for the population 18 years and older.

1. Hans-Dieter Klingemann and Charles Lewis Taylor, 'Affektive Parteiorientierung, Kanzlerkandidaten und Issues', in Max Kaase (ed.), *Wahlsoziologie heute* (Opladen: Westdeutscher Verlag, 1977), pp.301-47.
2. Wolfgang G. Gibowski and Max Kaase, 'Auf dem Weg zum politischen Alltag. Eine Analyse der ersten gesamtdeutschen Bundestagswahl vom 2. Dezember 1990', in *Aus Politik und Zeitgeschichte*, B 11-12/91, 8. März 1991, p.12.
3. Wolfgang G. Gibowski and Max Kaase, op cit., p.14.
4. 1992 saw the arrival of more than 430,000 asylum seekers and more than 230,000 ethnic German resettlers.
5. Wolfgang G. Gibowski and Max Kaase, op. cit., pp.10f.
6. Wolfgang G. Gibowski, 'Wie wirkt sich die wirtschaftliche Lage auf das Wahlverhalten aus', in Landeszentrale für politische Bildung Baden-Württemberg (ed.), *Wahlverhalten* (Stuttgart/Berlin/Köln: Kohlhammer Verlag, 1991), pp.122-38. Forschungsgruppe Wahlen e. V. Mannheim, *Politbarometer in Deutschland*, Dec. 1993 and Jan. 1994.
7. Matthias Jung and Dieter Roth, 'Kohls knappster Sieg. Eine Analyse der Bundestagswahl 1994', in *Aus Politik und Zeitgeschichte*, B 51-52/94, 23. Dez. 1994, pp.3-15.
8. Renate Köcher, 'Auf einer Woge der Euphorie. Veränderungen der Stimmungslage und des Meinungsklimas im Wahljahr 1994', in *Aus Politik und Zeitgeschichte*, B 51-52/94, 23. Dez. 1994, pp.16-21.
9. Result of the European Election of 12.06.1994: CDU-CSU 38.8%, + 1.0%; SPD 32.2%, - 5.1%; FDP 4.1%, -1.5%; Grüne 10.1%, +1.7%; REP 3.9%, -3.2%; PDS 4.7%, +4.7%; Others 6.3%, +2.6%.
10. Forschungsgruppe Wahlen e. V. Mannheim, *Blitzumfrage zur Bundestagswahl 1994*, Okt. 1994.
11. Infratest Burke Berlin, survey for *Die Zeit*, Feb. 1994.
12. Forschungsgruppe Wahlen e. V. Mannheim 'Sieg ohne Glanz: Eine Analyse der Bundestagswahl 1987', in Max Kaase and Hans-Dieter Klingemann (eds.), *Wahlen und Wähler. Analysen aus Anlaß der Bundestagswahl 1987* (Opladen: Westdeutscher Verlag, 1990), pp.689-734.
13. Carsten Bluck and Henry Kriekenbom, 'Die Wähler in der DDR: Nur issueorientiert oder auch parteigebunden?' in *Zeitschrift für Parlamentsfragen*, 22 (1991), pp.495-502. Gabriele Eckstein and Franz Urban Pappi, 'Die politischen Wahrnehmungen und die Präferenzen der Wählerschaft in Ost- und Westdeutschland: Ein Vergleich', in Hans-Dieter Klingemann and Max Kaase (eds.), *Wahlen und Wähler. Analysen aus Anlaß der Bundestagswahl 1990*

(Opladen: Westdeutscher Verlag, 1994), pp.397–421. Wolfgang G. Gibowski, 'Demokratischer (Neu)-Beginn in der DDR: Dokumentation und Analyse der Wahl vom 18. März 1990', in *Zeitschrift für Parlamentsfragen*, 21 (1990), pp.5–22.Wolfgang G. Gibowski and Max Kaase, op. cit., pp.3–20. Matthias Jung and Dieter Roth, 'Politische Einstellungen in Ost- und Westdeutschland seit der Bundestagswahl 1990', in *Aus Politik und Zeitgeschichte*, B 19/92, 1. Mai 1992, pp.3–16. Max Kaase and Hans-Dieter Klingemann, 'Der mühsame Weg zur Entwicklung von Parteiorientierungen in einer "neuen" Demokratie: Das Beispiel der früheren DDR', in Hans-Dieter Klingemann and Max Kaase (eds.), op. cit., pp.365–96. Hans Rattinger, 'Parteineigungen, Sachfragen- und Kanditatenorientierungen in Ost- und Westdeutschland 1990–1992', in Hans Rattinger, Oscar W. Gabriel and Wolfgang Jagodzinski (eds.), *Wahlen und politische Einstellungen im vereinigten Deutschland* (Bern/New York/Frankfurt/M.: Peter Lang, 1994), pp.267–314. Hans Rattinger, 'Parteiidentifikationen in Ost- und Westdeutschland nach der Vereinigung', in Oskar Niedermayer and Klaus von Beyme (eds.), *Politische Kultur in Ost- und Westdeutschland* (Berlin: Akademieverlag, 1994), pp.77–104. Holli A. Semetko and Klaus Schoenbach, *Germany's 'Unity Election'. Voters and the Media* (Cresskill, New Jersey: Hampton Press 1994).

14. Seymour M. Lipset and Stein Rokkan, 'Cleavage Structures, Party Systems and Voter Alignments: Introduction', in Seymour M. Lipset and Stein Rokkan (eds.), *Party Systems and Voter Alignments* (New York: Free Press, 1967), pp.1–64.

15. Wolfgang G. Gibowski, 'Demokratischer (Neu)-Beginn in der DDR'. See n.13.

16. Jürgen W. Falter and Markus Klein, 'Die Wähler der PDS bei der Bundestagswahl 1994. Ideologie und Protest', in *Aus Politik und Zeitgeschichte*, B 51-52/94, 23. Dez. 1994, pp.22–34.

SOURCES

Carsten Bluck and Henry Kreikenbom, 'Die Wähler in der DDR: Nur issueorientiert oder auch parteigebunden?', in *Zeitschrift für Parlamentsfragen*, 22 (1991), pp.495–502.

Gabriele Eckstein and Franz Urban Pappi, 'Die politischen Wahrnehmungen und die Präferenzen der Wählerschaft in Ost- und Westdeutschland: Ein Vergleich', in Hans-Dieter Klingemann and Max Kaase (eds.), *Wahlen und Wähler. Analysen aus Anlaß der Bundestagswahl 1990* (Opladen: Westdeutscher Verlag, 1994), pp.397–421.

Jürgen W. Falter and Markus Klein, 'Die Wähler der PDS bei der Bundestagswahl 1994. Ideologie, Nostalgie und Protest', in *Aus Politik und Zeitgeschichte*, B 51-52/94. (Dez. 1994), pp.22–34.

Forschungsgruppe Wahlen e. V. Mannheim, 'Gesamtdeutsche Bestätigung für die Bonner Regierungskoalition. Eine Analyse der Bundestagswahl 1990', in Hans-Dieter Klingemann and Max Kaase (eds.), op. cit., p.369.

Forschungsgruppe Wahlen e. V. Mannheim, 'Sieg ohne Glanz: Eine Analyse der Bundestagswahl 1987', in Max Kaase and Hans-Dieter Klingemann (eds.), *Wahlen und Wähler. Analysen aus Anlaß der Bundestagswahl 1987* (Opladen: Westdeutscher Verlag, 1990), pp.689–734.

Wolfgang G. Gibowski, 'Wie wirkt sich die wirtschaftliche Lage auf das Wahlverhalten aus', in Landeszentrale für politische Bildung Baden-Württemberg (ed.), *Wahlverhalten* (Stuttgart/Berlin/Köln: Kohlhammer Verlag, 1991), pp.122–38.

Wolfgang G. Gibowski, 'Demokratischer (Neu)-Beginn in der DDR: Dokumentation und Analyse der Wahl vom 18. März 1990', in *Zeitschrift für Parlamentsfragen*, 21 (1990), pp.5–22.

Wolfgang G. Gibowski and Max Kaase, 'Auf dem Weg zum politischen Alltag. Eine Analyse der ersten gesamtdeutschen Bundestagswahl vom 2. Dezember 1990', *in Aus Politik und Zeitgeschichte*, B 11-12/91 (8. März 1991), pp.3–20.

Matthias Jung and Dieter Roth, 'Politische Einstellungen in Ost- und Westdeutschland seit der Bundestagswahl 1990', in *Aus Politik und Zeitgeschichte*, B 19/92, (1. Mai 1992), pp.3–16.

Matthias Jung and Dieter Roth, 'Kohls knappster Sieg. Eine Analyse der Bundestagwahl 1994', in *Aus Politik und Zeitgeschichte*, B 51/52/94 (23. Dez. 1994), pp.3–15.

Max Kaase and Hans-Dieter Klingemann, 'Der mühsame Weg zur Entwicklung von Parteiorientierungen in einer 'neuen' Demokratie: Das Beispiel der früheren DDR', in Hans-Dieter Klingemann and Max Kaase (eds), op. cit., pp.365–96.

Hans-Dieter Klingemann and Charles Lewis Taylor, 'Affektive Parteiorientierung, Kanzlerkandidaten und Issues', in Max Kaase (ed.), *Wahlsoziologie heute* (Opladen: Westdeutscher Verlag (1977), pp.301–47.

Renate Köcher, 'Auf einer Woge der Euphorie. Veränderungen der Stimmungslage und des Meinungsklimas im Wahljahr 1994', in *Aus Politik und Zeitgeschichte*, B 51-52/94 (23. Dez. 1994), pp.16–21.

Seymour M. Lipset and Stein Rokkan: 'Cleavage Structures, Party Systems and Voter Alignments: Introduction', in Seymour M. Lipset and Stein Rokkan (eds.), *Party Systems and Voter Alignments* (New York: Free Press, 1967), pp.1–64.

Hans Rattinger, 'Parteiidentifikationen in Ost- und Westdeutschland nach der Vereinigung', in Oskar Niedermayer and Klaus von Beyme (eds.), *Politische Kultur in Ost- und Westdeutschland* (Berlin: Akademieverlag, 1994), pp.77–104.

Hans Rattinger, 'Parteineigungen, Sachfragen- und Kandidatenorientierungen in Ost- und Westdeutschland 1990–1992', in: Hans Rattinger, Oscar W. Gabriel and Wolfgang Jagodzinski (eds.), *Wahlen und politische Einstellungen im vereinigten Deutschland* (Bern/New York/Frankfurt/M.: Peter Lang, 1994), pp.267–314.

Holli A. Semetko and Klaus Schoenbach, 'Germany's "Unity Election". Voters and the Media' (Cresskill, New Jersey: Hampton Press 1994).

Candidates, Issues and Party Choice in the Federal Election of 1994

CARSTEN ZELLE

Utilising data from the 1994 Konrad Adenauer Foundation post-election survey, the relative importance of the chancellor-candidates, political issues and electoral partisanship are assessed in terms of their likely significance in influencing electoral choice in the Bundestag election. Reasons why such factors may have influenced electoral choice (and differences in the types of influence between east and west German electors) are considered.

The finish of the super-election race of 1994 was marked by a victory – though a narrow one – of the governing parties: Christian Democratic Union (CDU), its Bavarian counterpart Christian Social Union (CSU) and the coalition partner Free Democratic Party (FDP). The largest opposition party (Social Democratic Party, SPD) and its likely partner (Alliance 90/Greens) were unable to cash in on the lead the polls had given them throughout much of the period from 1991 to early 1994.

With this outcome a campaign had come to an end in which the two major parties had applied very different strategies. The CDU had run a highly candidate-centred campaign. Chancellor Helmut Kohl incorporated the message of (economic) optimism which was designed to draw voters from all ideological directions. Personalisation reached its height when a poster appeared in the 'hot phase' of the electoral battle which showed a photograph of Kohl amidst a crowd – without making any reference to his party, the CDU.[1] The SPD attempted to attract voters by employing a somewhat more traditional blend of campaign ingredients. The party focused on a number of issues and policy proposals, particularly – but not exclusively – on unemployment ('Jobs, Jobs, Jobs' read a major campaign slogan). Instead of featuring the contender for chancellor only, the campaign focused on the Troika, in which Scharping was joined (for example, on posters) by Oskar Lafontaine and Gerhard Schröder.[2] Voters, then, faced parties that tried to sell their messages in different political languages. On the one side there was Helmut Kohl, who was portrayed as a man who had delivered and who would continue to deliver if re-elected. The challenger, however, could not to the same degree only be viewed as an individual person. 'Kohl vs. the SPD' and 'the SPD vs. Kohl' probably better characterise this race than 'Kohl vs. Scharping' or 'CDU vs. SPD'.

This occurred at a time when there was a lot of talk of a growing influence of the candidates on electoral behaviour. In academia, the claim that the importance which contenders for chief of government in parliamentary systems bear for party choice was on the rise had been around for quite some time.[3] Although the empirical evidence to this effect was mixed at best in Germany,[4] the notion of *Persönlichkeitswahlen* (personality elections) was an often-heard *motif* in the interpretation of the 1994 elections. The elections in eastern Germany provided an additional boost to this hypothesis. It had long been suspected that voters in eastern Germany, who in large part lacked long-standing party affiliations, paid particular attention to the constellation of the candidates. The strong showings of 'King Kurt' Biedenkopf in Sachsen and Manfred Stolpe in Brandenburg were taken as cases in point. Despite the fact that they were prime ministers from different parties, both Biedenkopf and Stolpe were confirmed by absolute majorities in the neighbouring Länder in elections on the very same day, improving on their results in the previous elections. This defied any notion of a potential trend in favour of or against any particular party.

Against this backdrop the present survey article attempts to shed some light on candidates and issues in the federal election of 1994. How were the candidates for the office of chancellor viewed by the public? Which issues did the electorate think important, and which parties were perceived as the better 'problem solvers'? How important are candidates and issues for the electoral decision, and what is the role played by party attachments? Are there any indications of change?

The analysis employs the 1994 post-election survey conducted by the Department of Political Research of the Konrad Adenauer Foundation. A total of 4,000 respondents (2,500 in the west and 1,500 in the east) were interviewed between mid-November and late December. Fieldwork was conducted by Infratest-Burke.[5] Whenever percentages are reported, the data were weighted to reflect the population distribution in demographic variables and in party shares of the federal election. Correlation coefficients were calculated on the unweighted data set.

1. The Pull of the Candidates

Technically, voters choose a party in federal elections, not a chancellor. At the same time, the high visibility of the large parties' top candidates gives the voter the opportunity to make the *Kanzlerfrage* (chancellor question) a top concern for voting behaviour, as is frequently the case in parliamentary systems. Thus, it is not at all surprising that the winning candidate, Chancellor Helmut Kohl, is the one the plurality of voters preferred for the job: 46 per cent of the respondents who reported having voted preferred Kohl, 33 per cent chose Scharping. Of the rest, six per cent did not care and 15 per cent wanted neither candidate. These uncommitted groups were much larger in the east: a total of 30 per cent did not pick a candidate. Not surprisingly, a large chunk of those easterners who wanted neither candidate was composed of PDS voters (44 per cent). Among those who did report a preference, Kohl's lead was nearly as comfortable among eastern voters (11 points: 40 per cent Kohl and 29 per cent Scharping) as it was in the west (13 points: 47 per cent Kohl and 34 per cent Scharping).

What is it that made the voters prefer Kohl by such a margin? Figure 1, which plots the public images of the two candidates, offers some hints. Respondents were presented with a list of characteristics and then asked if an attribute fitted Kohl better, or Scharping. Kohl came out well ahead on a large number of items. Out of these, the silhouette of an active and experienced leader emerges. Thus, percentages between 37 and 65 saw Kohl rather than Scharping as 'energetic' and 'competent' and as having 'clear goals'. Among these attributes, the 65 per cent who described Kohl as having 'leadership qualities' constitute his strongest result. Scharping, in contrast, received percentages in the lower and upper tens for these attributes. Only seven per cent credit Scharping rather than Kohl with leadership qualities. The results are even more devastating for Scharping when experience and recognition were to be judged. Well aware that Scharping had little practice on the federal and the international stage, 82 per cent considered Kohl rather than Scharping as 'experienced'. Moreover 87 per cent regarded Kohl as the one who had 'international recognition'. The respective percentages for Scharping were minimal (experienced: three per cent, recognised: two per cent). All of these are professional characteristics, which a reasonable person may expect from a chancellor.

When it comes to human qualities, Scharping and Kohl generally do about equally well (or equally poorly). By and large, a fifth to a fourth of the population ascribe characteristics such as 'to the point', 'reliable', 'likeable' and 'humorous' to either candidate. Scharping scores an indisputable first place only for his 'social-mindedness'. 'Honesty' is a characteristic which a plurality of the respondents considers to apply to neither candidate (34 per cent for neither).

In sum, then, Kohl was preferred on the grounds of his favourable image with regard to professional qualities, while neither candidate scored major points for being the nicer guy. This public profile supports his 13-point lead over Scharping in chancellor preference. In the actual electoral returns, however, the governing coalition came out ahead by far less than this

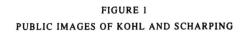

FIGURE 1
PUBLIC IMAGES OF KOHL AND SCHARPING

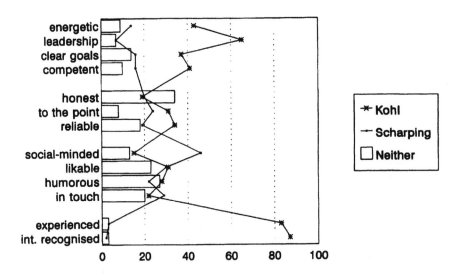

Source: Konrad Adenauer Foundation, post-election study 1994, Archive-No. 9401

margin. This is true regardless of which entities are chosen for comparison. Thus, the CDU–CSU led the SPD by 5.0 points, the coalition of CDU–CSU and FDP received 4.6 points more than SPD and Alliance 90/Greens, while its electorate was by only 0.2 points larger than the total support of the left parties (including the 4.4 per cent of the PDS). Obviously, the strong lead of the chancellor did not completely translate into electoral performance, because the candidate is only one of the factors influencing voters' choice.

This is not to say, however, that those who preferred Kohl were less likely to vote accordingly. In fact, among Kohl supporters the governing coalition received nine out of ten votes (see Table 1). The same holds true for Scharping supporters and the opposition parties of SPD and Alliance 90/Greens. There is no sign of a long-term trend in this connection: these percentages are in the neighbourhood of those reported by Norpoth for the elections between 1961 and 1976.[6]

In Kohl's case, there is no difference between east and west in this regard, while Scharping kept his support for SPD and Alliance 90/Greens at a higher margin in the west (93 per cent) than in the east (73 per cent). This is because 20 per cent of Scharping supporters in the east cast their vote in favour of the PDS. Nevertheless, when Germany as a whole is under

TABLE 1

ELECTORAL DECISION GIVEN PREFERENCE FOR A CERTAIN CHANCELLOR

Electoral Choice

	CDU-CSU or FDP	SPD or All./Greens	PDS	other
Chancellor preference				
Germany				
Kohl	91	7	1	2
Scharping	4	90	4	2
neither/both	25	51	14	11
West				
Kohl	91	7	-	2*
Scharping	4	93	-	3*
neither/both	29	55	-	16*
East				
Kohl	89	6	4	2
Scharping	4	73	20	3
neither/both	13	40	43	3

* = includes PDS

Source: Konrad Adenauer Foundation, Department of Political Research, post-election study 1994, Archive-No 9401

consideration there is no difference in the candidates' ability to keep the support they have for the parties that back them. Hence, the explanation for the fact that the government's lead is smaller than Kohl's cannot be sought among those who were committed to a candidate. Had only those respondents participated in the election, Kohl would have won by a larger margin.

Rather, the solution rests with those voters who did not prefer any candidate. With a combined SPD and Alliance 90/Greens share of 51 per cent, these voters disproportionally went to the opposition parties. The governing parties received only 25 per cent in this group. Among the eastern respondents in this group, the PDS attracted a plurality of the voters (43 per cent), closely followed by SPD and Alliance 90/Greens (40 per cent). The governing parties trailed at 13 per cent. Thus, the closeness of the final electoral result, which stands in contrast to Kohl's comfortable lead over Scharping in chancellor preference, is due to the relatively poor performance of the governing parties among those without a preference for chancellor. In the section dealing with political issues, this group will be examined more closely.

The results reported so far indicate that there is a strong relationship between chancellor preference and party choice on the individual level. Nevertheless, in the respondents' own assessment the candidate is not the overriding influence dominating the electoral decision. Granted, it is hardly feasible for the individual voter to be aware of the countless and complicated psychological mechanisms that affect the final choice. Therefore, a direct question should not be mistaken as a complete assessment of the candidates' effect. Rather it should be interpreted as only tapping the purely conscious component. Did the individual primarily vote for Kohl or Scharping, or did she/he opt for a certain party?

Thus asked, 22 per cent of the Germans named the candidates for chancellorship as their prime criterion. On the other hand, more than twice as many primarily chose a party (47 per cent), while 31 per cent spontaneously volunteered 'both to the same extent'. Perhaps surprisingly, the effect of the candidate is by no means assessed higher by eastern respondents. Instead, the overall percentages are strikingly similar, in no instance deviating more than one point between east and west. In sum, these numbers testify to a still overriding importance of the party. In the voters' own judgement, factors other than the candidate carry most of the weight of the electoral decision. At the same time, the results allow for a lesser, yet substantial, influence of the candidate.

Once again, the respondents' own assessment does not necessarily reflect the total magnitude of the candidate effect. Even when taking this problem of measurement into account, the instrument should be very powerful when comparing the pull of the candidates between different segments of society. Then, it is not so much the absolute magnitude of the candidate effect that is under scrutiny, but its variation between groups.[7]

This approach might be taken a little further in the quest for possible causes of candidate orientations in voting behaviour. Two contrasting models exist. On the one hand there is the claim that candidate orientation is a product of social change. This position holds that social strata that grew in size in the course of social modernisation on average put more emphasis on short-term factors (such as the person of the candidate) rather than focusing on the traditional profile of a party (as the party-loyals do). The major implication of this 'social view' is that candidate orientations became more frequent over time. Lacking the data to examine this implication directly, an indirect test can be conducted by comparing candidate orientations between different social strata. If modernised strata are more candidate-oriented, an increase of this type of voting behaviour is likely. The variables chosen for the test reported here are educational attainment and occupation. In this manner, the hypotheses that the better educated and the new middle classes are more prone to candidate-oriented voting behaviour than voters with less schooling and in other occupational groups can be tested. In order not to miss changes that exhibit themselves through generational change, candidate orientations will also be compared between age groups.

This 'social view' stands in opposition to the 'political view'. According to this perspective, the importance of the candidate for the voters is at least in part a reflection of the campaign's emphasis on the leading personnel. If the 'political view' is right, candidate orientations should be most pronounced among those voters who were particularly exposed to a candidate-centred campaign. In 1994, this is certainly true for CDU–CSU voters. Of course, the political view and the social view are not mutually exclusive.

The evidence compiled in Table 2 favours the political view over the social view. Conscious candidate orientations in voting behaviour are most frequent among voters of the CDU–CSU in the federal election of 1994 (29 per cent). Also, these are the voters which most frequently consider party and candidate as equally important for their electoral decision (37 per cent). The party was the prime concern for 34 per cent of CDU–CSU voters – 13 points less than in the entire sample. Interestingly, for the CDU–CSU there is the expected difference between voters in east and west, though it is not very large. In the west, party is considered more important than the candidate (by six points), while CDU–CSU supporters in the east are the only group for which candidates come out ahead (if only by two points). In contrast to the CDU–CSU supporters, voters of the other parties far more frequently mention 'party' as the overriding concern for the electoral decision. The percentages are 55 (SPD), 51 (FDP) and even 72 for the Alliance 90/Greens. Since the CDU campaign was the one which most heavily stressed the candidate, this finding is well in line with the political view.

How about the social view? According to this interpretation, candidate orientations gradually became more frequent because strata that expanded in the course of social modernisation – such as the well educated and the new middle classes – rely more heavily on persons. As the bottom sections of Table 2 reveal, this hypothesis is not supported by the empirical evidence. In fact, the opposite may well be true. The emphasis put on candidates is equal in different educational groups (21–22 per cent). In the east, it even becomes smaller as education increases (by five points), while in the west it is marginally more frequent among the better educated (by two points). More telling are the results regarding the 'parties' category: in both east and west party more frequently is the major criterion for the better educated than it is for those with less schooling. Thus, 53 per cent of the well educated in the west and 57 per cent of those in the east mention party, while respondents in the lowest educational category less frequently do so (43 per cent in the west, 42 per cent in the east). Accordingly, a mixed effect (both equally important) is reported more frequently by the less educated (36 per cent) than it is by those with higher educational attainment (24 per cent).

TABLE 2
SUBJECTIVE ASSESSMENT OF THE ROLE CANDIDATES AND PARTIES PLAY FOR THE ELECTORAL DECISION

	whole country larger role played by ...			West			East		
	Candidates	Parties	Equal	Candidates	Parties	Equal	Candidates	Parties	Equal
Total	22	47	31	22	47	31	21	47	32
Voted ...									
CDU-CSU	29	34	37	29	35	37	33	31	36
SPD	19	55	26	19	56	25	17	54	29
FDP	20	51	29	20	51	29	18	45	36
All. 90/Greens	11	72	17	12	71	17	5	77	18
PDS	-	-	-	-	-	-	8	67	24
Education:									
lower	22	43	36	21	43	36	23	42	35
intermediate	21	51	28	22	51	27	20	49	31
higher	22	53	24	23	53	24	18	57	25
Profession:									
worker	24	45	32	23	46	31	26	41	34
low to medium salariat	24	45	31	25	44	31	22	48	30
higher salariat	21	52	28	21	51	27	17	54	29
self-employed	22	41	37	23	41	36	19	42	39
Age:									
18-24 years	22	50	28	21	51	27	27	43	29
25-29 years	19	51	30	21	51	28	12	51	37
30-44 years	19	53	28	19	54	27	18	49	32
45-59 years	24	49	28	24	48	28	22	51	28
60 years and more	24	38	38	23	37	39	26	40	34

Source: Konrad Adenauer Foundation, post-election study 1994, Archive No.9401. Educational levels: lower = no degree, Hauptschule or Polytechnische Oberschule (POS) vor 10. Klasse; intermediate = Mittlere Reife or POS 10th degree; higher = at least Fachhochschulreife or Fachoberschule

For everything these subjective assessments can teach us, candidates play less of a role for the voting behaviour of the well educated than they do for the lesser educated. Thus, while there is evidence for important differences in candidate orientation between educational groups, these run counter to the expectations derived from the social modernisation perspective.

A similar conclusion emerges from the evidence in the occupational categories. As was the case for education, candidate orientations are equally frequent in all occupations – running counter to the social view. Moreover, the higher salariat – which is where a large part of the expanding new middle classes is located – puts the strongest emphasis on parties as the decisive factor in electoral decisions. In the east, the results are even clearer. The two categories of the salariat are the ones which put least emphasis on candidates and most emphasis on parties. Finally, a brief inspection of the respondents' age leads one to reject the notion that a gradual shift toward candidate oriented voting behaviour is taking place as a result of generational change. Instead, in the west emphasis on the parties decreases as one moves up the age groups. In the east, there is no clear relationship between candidate orientation and age.

In sum, these results flatly contradict the expectations of the social view. To the extent that it is possible to infer the existence of secular trends from cross-sectional analysis, one has to conclude that social change did not lead to an increase of candidate-oriented voting behaviour in Germany. By the same token, candidate orientations appear to be (partially) stimulated by candidate centred campaigns. 'The public responds to the political stimuli offered it', as Nie *et al.* concluded about the American electorate in 1976, appears to be an appropriate dictum in the present context as well.[8] As is the case when examining electoral volatility across countries, political factors appear to be much more powerful in explaining different patterns of electoral behaviour than social change is.[9] This finding is well in line with observations made in the United States, where both campaigns and voting behaviour became more personalised and therefore more volatile in the long run.[10] Tests more elaborate than are appropriate in a survey article will have to render a definitive judgement on this matter. What is at stake is the question whether political elites merely *react* to phenomena of electoral change which are beyond their control, or if parties and politicians potentially *produce* electoral change. If the political view is indeed accurate in the present context, changes in electoral behaviour may result if the personalised campaign continues to be employed.

2. Political Issues and Electoral Choice

Having inspected public opinion toward the candidates, the positions on political issues the parties and the electorate take constitute a second short-term factor influencing the distribution of party support. In the super-election year, the parties faced a public opinion that was dominated by concerns of economic and material well-being. In fact, a common political agenda had developed in the united Germany during the years after unification. Ranked by the percentage that considered an issue 'very important', unemployment led the list throughout 1993 and 1994 in east and west. Other issues in top places were the economy, the social system, retirement funds and crime.[11]

As can be seen from Table 3, this emphasis on economic issues remained unchanged after the federal election. Still, unemployment is the undisputed leader on the list in both parts of the country, followed by the economy. The social system remains among the leading four, albeit 'securing the retirement funds' slipped to sixth place in the east, while it is third in the west. 'World peace', which had not been included on the list in the last years, appears at third place in the east and fourth in the west. 'Crime' is

TABLE 3

TOP POLITICAL PRIORITIES 1994/1995

Total	West	East	CDU-CSU-Voters	SPD-Voters
1. Jobs (84 %)	1. Jobs (83 %)	1. Jobs (91 %)	1. Jobs (85 %)	1. Jobs (88 %)
2. Economy (77 %)	2. Economy (75 %)	2. Economy (84 %)	2. Economy (79 %)	2. Social system (78 %)
3. Retirement funds (75 %)	Retirement funds (75 %)	3. Social system (83 %)	3. Retirement funds (78 %)	Retirement funds (78 %)
4. Social system (74 %)	4. Social system (72 %)	World peace (83 %)	4 World peace (75 %)	4. Economy (76 %)
World peace (74 %)	World peace (72 %)	5. Crime (80 %)	5. Crime (73 %)	World peace (76 %)
6. Right-wing extremism (69 %)	6. Right-wing extremism (67 %)	6. Retirement funds (79 %)	6. Social system (69 %)	6. Right-wing extremism (71 %)
7. Crime (68 %)	7. Env.Protection (66 %)	7. Right-wing extremism (77 %)	Right-wing extremism (69 %)	7. Housing (69 %)
8. Env. Protection (65 %)	8. Crime (65 %)	8. Equal living conditions East-West (75 %)	8. Political radicalism (67 %)	8. Families and children (68 %)
Housing (65 %)				

Source: Konrad Adenauer Foundation, Department of Political Research, post-election study 1994, Archive No. 9401

considered more important by the eastern population (fifth compared to eighth), while right-wing extremism assumes neighbouring positions (west: sixth, east: seventh). Having been the most important issues in the view of west Germans in 1990, environmental protection is positioned seventh in the west now, while it is only 13th in the east.[12] In return, 'bringing about equal living conditions in east and west' ranks higher for east German citizens. In sum, then, with a few notable exceptions a common political agenda continued to be in place. The large parties took advantage of this fact when they designed their campaigns around the leading issues. There was only limited necessity to apply different electoral strategies in east and west.

Interestingly, the electorates of the large parties deviate to a slightly larger extent from each other in the rankings of political priorities than the eastern and western populations do. To be sure, unemployment most frequently was judged very important by the supporters of both CDU–CSU and SPD. In second place – which is the economy for the CDU–CSU and the social system for the SPD – the traditional differences in political focus become apparent, though. The same holds true for the issue of crime, which ranks fifth for CDU–CSU voters, while it is in 11th place for the SPD electorate. Not surprisingly, voters' issue positions and the large parties' traditional profiles correspond to a large extent.

In order for the political issues to help us to understand electoral decisions, the perceived competence of the parties to solve a problem has to be taken into account. After all, being the party perceived to be more competent to solve an important problem is the goal of an electoral campaign – at least to the extent that the campaign talks about issues. Traditionally, Germans regarded the SPD as most competent to solve the problem of unemployment, while the CDU–CSU mostly has been viewed as the party to get the economy going. In 1994, public opinion made some interesting changes in this connection. In early 1994, the SPD was well ahead on unemployment, but at the same time was head to head with the CDU–CSU when it came to the economy. In the course of the year, the CDU–CSU continuously made inroads on both issues. In the west, it regained its lead regarding economic issues in March. In the east, the pendulum shifted toward the CDU–CSU in May. By the end of the year, the party had a comfortable lead of more than 20 points in economic competence.[13] In the data set under study here, the CDU–CSU was perceived as more competent for solving economic problems by a margin of 35 per cent in the west and 26 per cent in the east (see Table 4).

But what about the number one issue: unemployment? Presumably, this issue was the one with the highest potential to affect electoral decisions in 1994. As it turns out, in our survey neither party has a substantial lead on this issue. Overall, the CDU–CSU is barely ahead (by two points). In the

TABLE 4

PERCEIVED COMPETENCE TO SOLVE PROBLEMS (CDU–CSU:SPD)

Difference in percentage points

	Germany	West	East	Candidate pref: neither or both
Jobs	+ 2	+ 5	- 9	- 19
Economy	+33	+35	+26	+20
Retirement funds	- 1	- 2	+ 4	- 22
Social system	- 23	- 24	- 21	- 39
World peace	+10	+11	+ 5	- 4
Right-wing extremism	+ 5	+ 7	- 4	- 4
Crime	+20	+24	+ 5	+10
Env. protection	- 3	- 3	- 3	- 13
Housing	- 13	- 13	- 13	- 31
Equal living conditions	+ 9	+12	- 4	- 6

Source: Konrad Adenauer Foundation, Department of Political Research, post-election study 1994, Archive No. 9401

west, the edge is a little bit more pronounced (five points), while in the east it is reversed into a somewhat more substantial advantage for the SPD (nine points). This situation marks the end of a trend that could be observed throughout 1994. The initial SPD advantage on the number one issue, which the party emphasised heavily in its campaign ('Arbeit, Arbeit, Arbeit'), steadily slipped away.

As for the number four issue, the social system, the SPD's lead was unchallenged. The party came out well ahead on this issue in both west (by 24 points) and east (21 points). Among the remaining issues, the CDU–CSU's lead on crime (20 points) and the SPD's edge on housing (13 points) constitute the most noteworthy results. All in all, public opinion appeared very much to be in two minds about which party to prefer on account of the political issues. SPD and CDU–CSU were even on the issues ranked first and third, the CDU had a strong lead on the second most important, while the SPD came out well ahead on the fourth most important. Still, when considering the list in its entirety, the CDU–CSU had a slight edge.

As pointed out in the section on the candidates, all indications are that the CDU–CSU did very well among the sizeable portion of voters who favoured Kohl for chancellor, while doing relatively poorly among those voters who did not prefer one candidate over the other. The last column in Table 4 lists the perceived competencies of the large parties among the voters not committed to either Kohl or Scharping. Not being exposed to candidate influences on vote choice, the issue profile of these respondents renders it easily understandable why most of them favoured the opposition parties. In this group, the CDU–CSU is more frequently than the SPD perceived as competent only for the issues of the economy and crime. Moreover, compared to the sample as a whole, the distance to the SPD is much smaller in these cases. For the bulk of the issues the SPD is perceived as better suited to solve a problem. This includes the most important issue: unemployment, on which the SPD has a 19-point lead over the CDU–CSU among respondents without candidate preference. Assuming that the voters lacking a clear candidate cue to party choice voted on the basis of the issues, an electoral outcome closely resembling the actual result makes good sense in light of these data.

3. Candidates, Issues, Partisanship: Estimating their Independent Effects

The empirical evidence presented so far leaves little doubt that *both* candidates and political issues are related to party choice in the federal election of 1994 in an important manner. But just how important are they? Did the voters in the federal election for the most part choose between personalities? Or did they primarily evaluate the parties on the basis of their perceived competence? To what extent are the two factors interconnected? And what is the role party identification plays?

Unfortunately, it is generally hardly feasible to answer these questions in a more or less definitive way. The countless attempts to disentangle the individual contributions which parties, issues and candidates make to individual electoral behaviour fill a long chapter in the history of electoral research. All of them had to wrestle with the fact that political attitudes are heavily interrelated, making it hard to disentangle individual relationships once others are controlled. Yet, what is usually considered a problem for analysis can also be viewed as an important finding: in most cases, voters choose the party which they prefer on account of party allegiance, issue positions and candidate evaluations simultaneously. However, what is truly problematic is that this homogeneity of political attitudes makes it hard to investigate possible causal connections in the cross-section. For instance, the question to what extent a certain candidate preference causes voters to choose that party, and to what extent voters prefer pretty much any candidate nominated by the party they feel attached to anyway is yet to be answered.[14]

Even in light of these limitations, electoral research has produced a number of notable results with respect to the factors influencing individual voting behaviour in Germany. By and large, the effect of candidates and issues for party choice is considered low to moderate at best once party identification is controlled.[15] Even so, it is frequently pointed out that these short-term factors may easily tip the balance in any given election. Also, most analysts concur in the finding that candidates are more important for the electoral decision than are issues and the parties' competencies.[16] Thus, candidates are generally viewed as the second most important factor influencing the electoral choice, after party identification. Moreover, Rattinger found that for eastern respondents candidate orientations are even more important in maintaining the evaluation of a party over time than party identification is.[17] Most probably, findings like these were among the motives for the parties, and most of all the CDU, to put extraordinary emphasis on the candidates in the electoral campaign of 1994.

Which factors influenced party choices in the federal election of 1994? In Table 5 coefficients are listed which tap the relationship between a political attitude and the vote (Pearson's r). A large coefficient (close to 1.0) indicates that the attitude under study is strongly related to party choice (CDU–CSU v. SPD). Smaller coefficients (approaching 0) signify that party choice and the political attitude exist independently of each other. Negative values of r (approaching -1.0) indicate the unlikely situation that party choice on average runs counter to the direction of a political attitude. A quick glance at Table 5 makes clear that this is the case for none of the attitudes under study here. Hence, on average, citizens hold favourable attitudes of the party they voted for with respect to each item: candidates, issues and party attachment.

The coefficients support the notion that each of these: candidates, issues and party attachments, is important for vote choice in the federal election of 1994. Judging from these individual relationships, party attachments are the single most important factor influencing electoral decisions in both east and west (r = .83 in the west and .79 in the east).[18] With regard to the remaining factors, there appears to be no more than a marginal difference in the importance of candidates and issue competencies of the large parties. Evaluations of the candidates are correlated at .73 (west) and .71 (east) with party choice.[19] A combined issue scale, which summarises competence perceptions of ten issues, yields a correlation of .74 in the west and .69 in the east.[20] Judging from the results of this first attempt to compare the weight candidates and issues carry for the electoral decision on the individual level, both appear to be of about equal importance. Also, there is no sign of differences between east and west in how these criteria are applied to the electoral decision.

Before moving on in the investigation of this question, it is useful briefly to consider how the parties' perceived competence on the individual issues relate to the vote. When the components of the issue scale are regarded individually, it turns out that in the west the problems that the priority ranking features in the top places are also the ones which are most closely

TABLE 5

CANDIDATES, ISSUES AND PARTIES: THEIR RELATION TO ELECTORAL
BEHAVIOUR. BIVARIATE CORRELATIONS WITH THE VOTE FOR THE
LARGE PARTIES (0 = SPD, 1 = CDU–CSU)

	West	East
Candidates		
Feeling thermometer		
(Kohl - Scharping)	.73	.71
Issue competence		
(CDU–CSU - SPD)		
Jobs	.63	.49
Economy	.61	.52
Retirement funds	.62	.58
Social system	.61	.52
World peace	.54	.45
Right-wing	.43	.41
Crime	.48	.51
Environment	.50	.43
Combined issue scale	.74	.69
Party identification		
(0 = SPD, 1 = None or		
other, 2 = CDU-CSU)	.83	.79

Source: Konrad Adenauer Foundation, Department of Political Research, post-election study
1994, Archive No. 9401

related to the electoral decision. Each of the top four issues (jobs, economy,
retirement funds, and social system) yields a correlation in the lower sixties
with the vote for the large parties. The issues ranked lower in importance
also bear a little less significance in separating CDU–CSU voters from SPD
voters. Thus, not only did public opinion put less stress on issues such as
world peace, right-wing extremism, crime and the environment, but the
individual decisions between the large parties also took them into account
to a lesser extent (r ranging from .43 to .54). Among east Germans, the
situation was different. Here, the correlation of party competence to the vote
stands in no apparent connection to the importance of an issue in the public
judgement. Moreover, all but one out of the eight issues listed here correlate
a little less strongly with the vote in the east than in the west, the exception
being the issue of crime. This result poses something of a puzzle. However,
it may very well be due to the fact that the third largest party in the east, the
PDS, is not included in the present analysis.

Back to the original question. So far, it was demonstrated that when the
factors influencing the electoral decision are investigated one by one,
candidates and issues appear to be equally important. Treating these
attitudes as if their impact on the decision process occurred independently

of the others, however, quite obviously misses reality. After all, it is most unlikely that competence perceptions should not in one way or another be affected by a sense of party allegiance, and the same holds true for candidate evaluations. To the extent that these kinds of interrelationships exist, examining the variables' relationships to the vote without taking into account the role of the others almost certainly leads to 'double-counting' of certain effects. It is of central relevance for the understanding of electoral behaviour to learn how much a certain attitude contributed to the final decision between the parties once the other factors are accounted for. Technically speaking, the independent effects of the attitudes under study are to be examined and compared.

A straightforward statistical tool to get a rough idea of the contribution the various attitudes make when controlled for the others is multiple regression analysis. Regression coefficients (beta weights) represent the linear combination of the presumed causal variables that best accounts for the variance between the numerous party choices on the individual level. However, once the hypothesised causal factors are substantially correlated with each other (as is the case in the present analysis), much care has to be applied when interpreting these coefficients. Nevertheless, they can offer valuable hints, particularly when viewed in connection with additional pieces of evidence.

The regression equation compiled in Table 6 shows once more that partisanship is the most influential of the three factors influencing electoral choice. The beta weight of the general attachment to a party is a substantial .55 in the west and .50 in the eastern sample. As suggested by earlier results, it appears that the German voters in the first place chose *parties* in the federal election of 1994. The evaluation of Kohl and Scharping emerges as the second most important predictor of the electoral decision. The respective beta weights are substantially higher than those for the combined issue scale. What is more, the coefficient for candidate evaluations is a little larger in the east (.29) than it is in the west (.22). In contrast to the findings derived with the direct question, this result conforms with the notion that candidate oriented voting behaviour perhaps is more common in the new Länder. Finally, of all the attitudes under consideration, issue orientations exhibit the weakest independent influence on party choice in both west (.15) and east (.13). Taken together, the three variables explain most of the variance in voting behaviour for the two large parties (west: 73 per cent, east 69 per cent).

Evidence of another kind supports the thesis that voters on average weighted the political attitudes in the order: parties, candidates, issues when making a choice in the federal election of 1994. The regression coefficients considered above represent the individual factors' weight in what the

TABLE 6

ESTIMATING THE INDEPENDENT EFFECTS OF CANDIDATES: ISSUES
AND PARTY IDENTIFICATION

	independent effect (beta)		% of voting behaviour solely due to individual factor (R^2-reduction* 100)	
	West	East	West	East
Candidates	.22	.29	2	4
Issues	.15	.13	1	1
Party identification	.55	.50	11	11
%-Variance explained by all three together (R^2 * 100)			73	69

all beta coefficients significant at .0000

Source: Konrad Adenauer Foundation, Department of Political Research, post-election study 1994, Archive No. 9401

statistical procedure delivered as the equation best fitting the empirical data. Since the factors are interrelated, these coefficients are not necessarily inaccurate, but they are certainly error-prone to a high degree. Therefore, the variance of any one of the three factors that is indispensable to arrive at the best explanation has been calculated. This number represents a factor's unique contribution to the understanding of the electoral decision, that is that contribution none of the remaining variables could have added.[21]

As it turns out, none of the three factors: parties, candidates, issues provides unique explanatory power to a very large extent. Rather, with the unique contribution ranging from one per cent to 11 per cent, the bulk of the electoral decision is accounted for by variance that is shared between the three types of attitudes. In light of what was said earlier, this is not surprising. Attachments to the parties, evaluations of the candidates, and perceptions of the parties' competence to solve political problems heavily depend on each other. In most cases, an electoral decision is simultaneously carried by supporting attitudes on all three of those factors. Hence, it is not possible to sort out the relative weight of any one of these factors for the majority of the sample.

Nevertheless, cross-sectional research into the factors influencing party choice can provide some additional insights. In fact, one might argue that since the analysis rests heavily on those voters who hold attitudes that are not perfectly in accordance with each other with regard to which party is favoured, it concentrates on the voters who are most likely to actually make a choice in an election, rather than merely casting a vote for the party that one prefers no matter what. Thus, one might speculate that this type of analysis is focused on the citizens who may or may not produce change in electoral returns.

Be that as it may, party once again emerges as the top influence on the electoral decision, with a unique contribution of 11 per cent in east and west. Candidates are second. Remarkably, once again candidates appear to carry more weight in the east, where they deliver a unique contribution of four per cent, than in the west, where the respective value is two per cent. Issues finish last, contributing one per cent to the explanation of the electoral decision in both east and west. Hence, when the three types of attitudes do not favour the same party, voters in the federal election of 1994 apparently considered the party in the first place, then the candidate, and only lastly the perceived competencies of the parties on political issues. Among east German voters, the candidate was more important for the electoral decision than in the west.

4. Conclusions

This article investigated how the candidates for chancellor and the political issues were viewed by the German electorate, and how important each was for party choice at the federal election of 1994. Most of the analysis and discussion was limited to the CDU–CSU and the SPD. With respect to public opinion at election time, three rather clear results can be noted:

1. Kohl had a comfortable lead over Scharping in chancellor preference. This was due to the favourable judgement the public rendered on his professional qualities and on his experience. With respect to human qualities, Kohl and Scharping were evaluated about equally.

2. The election year was dominated by economic issues, and most of all unemployment, in both parts of the country alike. Both parties took advantage of this by making these issues central elements of their campaigns in east and west. All in all, perceived issue competencies to solve the problems slightly favoured the CDU–CSU in east and west.

3. The segment of the electorate not indicating any preference for the chancellor overwhelmingly voted for the opposition parties. This corresponds with the favourable competence profile on political issues the SPD had with these voters. This explains why Kohl's lead over Scharping did not translate into an equally wide margin of the government parties in the electoral outcome.

Due to the nature of an early survey article, analyses of other questions could not be taken to the point where a more or less definitive judgement could be reached. Yet, a number of tentative theses emerge from the discussion. Being preliminary in character, all of these deserve further scrutiny.

4. In the electorate's own assessment, the candidate plays a substantial, but by no means a major, role for the electoral decision. If candidate oriented voting behaviour became more frequent over time – as some claim it did – there is no evidence to the effect that this resulted from social change. In contrast to this 'social view' stands the 'political view', which identifies the types of campaign styles as influencing voting behaviour. In this view, the degree to which voters use the candidate to arrive at a party choice varies in accordance with the emphasis the campaign had put on it. This view receives some support in the data. If the political view is indeed accurate – as more elaborate future tests will have to investigate – changing campaign styles are a potential cause, not an effect, of electoral change.

5. For the most part, individuals hold party attachments, perceived issue competencies and candidate evaluations that each favour one and the same party. Where this is not the case, party attachments played the largest role in influencing electoral decisions. The second most important factor was the candidates. Political issues influenced party choice less strongly.

6. The evidence is contradictory when the weight of the candidates for the electoral decision is compared between voters in east and west Germany. In subjective assessments, there is no difference in candidate orientations between east and west. When the electoral decision is modelled, however, the candidates appear of more importance in the east.

NOTES

1. For an account of the CDU campaign see Christopher Anderson and Carsten Zelle, 'Helmut Kohl and the CDU Victory', in Russell J. Dalton and Andrei Markovits (eds.), *German Politics and Society Special Issue: Bundestagswahl 1994*, Vol.13, No.1 (1995), pp.12–35.
2. For the SPD campaign see Gerard Braunthal, 'The Left Parties in the 1994 Election', in Dalton and Markovits (eds.), *Bundestagswahl 1994*, pp.36–49.
3. David Butler and Donald Stokes, *Political Change in Britain* (New York: St. Martin's Press, 1971); Helmut Norpoth, 'Kanzlerkandidaten. Wie sie vom Wähler bewertet werden und wie sie die Wahlentscheidung beeinflussen', in Max Kasse (ed.), *Wahlsoziologie heute. Analysen aus Anlass der Bundestagswahl 1976* (Opladen: Westdeutscher Verlag, 1977), p.568; Clive Bean and Anthony Mughan, 'Leadership Effects in Parliamentary Elections in Australia and

CANDIDATES, ISSUES AND PARTY CHOICE   73

Britain', *American Political Science Review*, Vol.83, No.4 (1989), pp.1165–80.
4. Max Kaase, 'Is There Really Personalization in Politics? Candidates and Voting Behaviour in Germany in Dynamic Perspective' (paper presented at the annual meeting of the American Political Science Association, Sept. 1993, Washington D.C.); Jürgen Lass, *Kandidatenorientierung und Wahlverhalten* (Dissertation Free University Berlin, 1993).
5. I wish to thank the Infratest office in Berlin for being very helpful in making the data available as early as possible.
6. Helmut Norpoth, 'Kanzlerkandidaten. Wie sie vom Wähler bewertet werden und wie sie die Wahlentscheidung beeinflussen', in Max Kaase (ed.), *Wahlsoziologie heute. Analysen aus Anlaß der Bundestagswahl 1976* (Opladen: Westdeutscher Verlag, 1977), p.564.
7. This is assuming that measurement error and conceptual weaknesses are not related to the grouping variables examined in the following.
8. Norman Nie, Sidney Verba and John R. Petrocik, *The Changing American Voter* (Cambridge, Mass.: Harvard University Press, 1976), p.319.
9. See Carsten Zelle, *Der Wechselwähler, Eine Gegenüberstellung politischer und sozialer Erklärungsansätze des Wählerwandels in Deutschland und den USA* (Opladen: Westdeutscher Verlag, 1995).
10. Cf. Leon Epstein, *Political Parties in the American Mold* (Madison: University of Wisconsin Press, 1986); Martin P. Wattenberg, *The Decline of American Political Parties 1952–1994* (Cambridge, Mass.: Harvard University Press, 1994); Zelle, op. cit.
11. See Hans-Joachim Veen and Carsten Zelle, 'National Identity and Political Priorities in Eastern and Western Germany', *German Politics*, Vol.4, No.1 (1995), pp.1–26.
12. The fact that in the east all issues yield higher percentages for 'very important' does not interfere with these conclusions. This type of behaviour has repeatedly been observed with east Germans. See Helmut Jung, *Neue Märkte im Osten: sozialer und politischer Wandel und neue Konsumgewohnheiten in den neuen Bundesländern* (Frankfurt/Dresden: Basisresearch, 1992).
13. See the data reported by the institute EMNID.
14. But see Benjamin I. Page and Calvin C. Jones, 'Reciprocal Effects of Policy Preference, Party Loyalties and the Vote', *American Political Science Review*, Vol.73, No.4 (1979), pp.1071–89; Morris P. Fiorina, *Retrospective Voting in American National Elections* (New Haven: Yale University Press, 1981) for attempts to do so in the American case.
15. See Helmut Norpoth, 'Kanzlerkandidaten. Wie sie vom Wähler bewertet werden und wie sie die Wahlentscheidung beeinflussen', in Max Kaase (ed.), *Wahlsoziologie heute. Analysen aus Anlaß der Bundestagswahl 1976* (Opladen: Westdeuscher Verlag, 1977), pp.551–72; Hans-Dieter Klingemann and Charles L. Taylor, 'Affektive Parteiorientierung, Kanzlerkandidaten und Issues. Einstellungskomponenten der Wahlentscheidung bei Bundestagswahlen in Deutschland', in Max Kaase (ed.), *Wahlsoziologie heute. Analysen aus Anlaß der Bundestagswahl 1976* (Opladen: Westdeutscher Verlag, 1977), pp.301–47; Jürgen W. Falter and Hans Rattinger, 'Parteien, Kandidaten und politische Streitfragen bei der Bundestagswahl 1980: Möglichkeiten und Grenzen der Normal-Vote-Analyse', in Max Kaase and Hans-Dieter Klingemann (eds.), *Wahlen und politisches System. Analysen aus Anlaß der Bundestagswahl 1980* (Opladen: Westdeutscher Verlag, 1983), pp.320–421.
16. Klingemann and Taylor, op. cit.; Falter and Rattinger op. cit.: see most recently Hans Rattinger, 'Parteineigungen, Sachfragen- und Kandidatenorientierungen in Ost- und Westdeutschland 1990–1992', in Hans Rattinger, Oscar W. Gabriel and Wolfgang Jagodzinski (eds.), *Wahlen und politische Einstellungen im vereinigten Deutschland* (Frankfurt et al.: Peter Lang, 1994), pp.267–315.
17. Rattinger, op. cit.
18. Party attachments were measured by asking the respondents if, generally speaking, they tended to one party more than the others. This is the standard question to tap the German equivalent of party identification. Though the measure is well established, there are doubts regarding its stability. For a discussion see for example Peter Gluchowski, 'Parteiidentifikationen im politischen System der Bundesrepublik Deutschland. Zum Problem der empirischen Überprüfung eines Konzepts unter variierten Systembedingungen', in Dieter Oberndörfer (ed.), *Wählerverhalten in der Bundesrepublik Deutschland* (Berlin:

Duncker & Humblot, 1978), pp.265–323.

19. The candidate evaluation scale was constructed by subtracting the 11-point feeling thermometer for Scharping from that for Kohl. The resulting scale ranges from -10 to +10, with positive values indicating preference for Kohl.

20. This scale was constructed as follows: each respondent was assigned a value of 1 when the CDU/CSU was mentioned, -1 for when the SPD was mentioned, and 0 if both parties, other parties or no parties were mentioned on the competence variable for the ten most important issues. Then, each competence variable was weighted by how important the respondent judged the respective issue to be (0 = not important, 1 = less important, 2 = rather important, 3 = very important). These scores were added to yield the combined issue scale.

21. The measure employed here is the reduction in R^2 when the factor under study is omitted from the equation. This technique resembles the one employed by Falter and Rattinger, op. cit., pp.403–8.

Superwahljahr in the New Länder: Polarisation in an Open Political Market

STEPHEN PADGETT

Four years after unification, the 1994 elections in the new Länder show the institutional weakness of the parties, an electorate relatively unstructured by group based partisanship, and a party system characterised by potentially unstable structures of party competition. Whilst party membership has stabilised, there is little indication that the post-unification decline can be reversed. Although group partisanship 'normalised' somewhat in 1994 it remains weaker than in the west, with a correspondingly higher incidence of 'situational' voting and more electoral volatility. Tendencies towards concentration and polarisation mean that the party system is less predictable than previously, with a more open political market in which the capacity of the parties to control politics is significantly reduced.

Successive elections in the new German Länder in 1990 left some major questions unanswered. Firstly, introduced by institutional transfer, the parties lacked the organic social roots of their counterparts in the west. Although the party landscape resembled that of western Germany, its underlying resilience was uncertain. Secondly, it was impossible to discern with any degree of confidence whether election results reflected permanent patterns of partisanship, or merely a snapshot of political opinion under the unique circumstances of unification. A third question related to a party system which was less concentrated than in the west, and which contained five parties rather than four. Whilst the 1990 elections provided a sound foundation for coalition formation at both federal and Land levels, party system dynamics were unpredictable. The 1994 elections provide evidence from which these questions may be answered. The following analysis examines this evidence against the background of developments in the party landscape since 1990, and draws some conclusions about party system dynamics in the new Länder.

The Party Landscape

Organisational Density

Established with extreme rapidity during a period of acute social and political upheaval, the parties in the new Länder lacked secure institutional foundations. The origins of the CDU and FDP were in the reformed remnants of the GDR block parties, whilst the SPD emerged from the opposition movements in the last months of the old regime. Rapid merger with counterparts in the west provided immediate access to an organisational apparatus which buttressed the tenuous existence of the fledgling eastern parties. The introduction by institutional transfer of a 'ready made' western-style party system contributed greatly to the political integration of the two parts of Germany, and was sanctioned by the electorate in December 1990. Because the parties were largely exogenous to eastern German society, however, their social roots were shallow, and organisational infrastructures weak. In particular, the low membership of the major parties cast doubt on their long-term resilience.

As can be seen from Table 1, the organisational density of the major parties lies well below western levels. All parties have suffered a dramatic decline in membership since 1990, and whilst this had stabilised by 1994, there was little indication of a significant new growth potential. In the CDU and FDP, decline reflects the large-scale withdrawal of members inherited from their block party predecessors. These elements made up 70 per cent of the CDU's 134,000 members in 1990,[1] and remain a majority of the party's reduced membership. The FDP was even more heavily dominated by elements inherited from predecessor parties, accounting for around 90 per cent of party membership.[2] The largest of the parties is the PDS with a membership of around 130,000 in 1994. It has been estimated that 95 per cent of PDS members belonged to the SED.[3] Of the larger parties, only the SPD was genuinely new. Early estimates of 100,000 members were based on attendance at inaugural meetings or signatures of support, and proved inauthentic. With the introduction of proper membership accounting, the figure fell sharply to 22,000 in mid-1991, recovering to 27,000 by 1994.[4] The other new party, Bündnis 90/Die Grünen, had only 3,800 members in 1994.[5]

There are a number of explanations for low and declining party membership. First, in the old regime party affiliation was largely opportunistic: SED membership was accompanied by a range of privileges, whilst the block parties provided a political and social niche, apart from the SED, yet officially sanctioned. Parties in a liberal democracy offer fewer material and social rewards. Moreover, the GDR experience casts a pejorative shadow over party activity. Second, the material and psycho-

TABLE 1
PARTY MEMBERSHIP AND ORGANISATIONAL DENSITY EAST GERMAN LÄUDER
(DATE IN PARENTHESES)

	CDU	SPD	FDP	PDS	B90/G
Brandenburg	10,707	6,461	4,700	36,000	–
	(8.93)	(9.93)	(9.93)	(6.91)	
Sachsen-Anhalt	16,500	5,491	7,200	19,470	–
	(3.94)	(1.94)	(1.94)	(3.94)	–
Sachsen	23,495	5,190	7,400	34,294	–
	(6.94)	(1.94)	(1.94)	(9.94)	
Thüringen	20,341	5,954	7,841	16,530	–
	(7.94)	(9.94)	(1.93)	(9.94)	
Mecklenburg-	10,500	3,287	7,836	30,813	–
Vorpommern	(12.93)	(12.91)	(12.91)	(3.91)	
E Germany ex E Berlin	81,543	26,383	34,977	137,107	3,800
Membership E	2.5	1.0	11.5	8.1	0.8
as % of electorate W	5.1	6.1	2.2	–	1.2

Source: Party *Landesgeschäftsstellen*

logical insecurity accompanying the upheaval of unification, it has been argued, has led to an individualistic preoccupation with private affairs, discouraging participation in public life. A third explanation is rooted in political culture theory: the discrepancy between the passive 'subject culture' of post-communist society and the participatory 'civic culture' of liberal democracy.[6] Finally, it could be argued that the nature of the *Wende* prejudiced party formation. The decisive force in the collapse of the GDR was spontaneous protest rather than organised opposition. In the absence of organised movements, and with parties introduced by organisational transfer, the disjuncture between democratisation and party formation meant that the political dynamism of the *Wende* failed to sustain the process of party building.

Organisational Capacity

The low organisational density of the parties in the new Länder severely limits their organisational capacity. In the absence of a large-scale membership, the dense organisational structures characteristic of parties in western Germany are difficult to sustain. The CDU and SPD are structured according to the west German model: Landesverbände subdivided into Kreisverbände/Unterbezirke, with Ortsvereine representing the party grassroots. The SPD, however, has had to adjust the model to allow for low membership: Unterbezirke cover a wider geographical area, and there are proportionally fewer Ortsvereine (around 1,300 as against 10,000 in the west). Nevertheless, outside the cities local party activity is tenuous: in Sachsen 43 per cent of SPD Ortsvereine have less than ten members.[7] The federal structure of the FDP gives the Landesverbände greater organisational flexibility: in Sachsen-Anhalt the party has dispensed with Ortsvereine and is simply subdivided into 40 Kreisverbände varying in membership from 50 to 400.[8] The larger membership of the PDS enables it to maintain a more intensive local organisation than its competitors. The Sachsen-Anhalt party, for instance has 975 Basisgruppen, with an average of 20 members in each.[9] In part, the organisational weakness of the parties in the east is offset by a higher than usual level of member-activism. Nevertheless, apart from the PDS, organisational structures at local level remain extremely weak.

A shortfall of membership revenue also means that party organisations in the east are much less professionalised than their western counterparts. Only the CDU maintains more than a skeletal professional staff. Very heavily supported from Bonn, the CDU employs around 300 officials, with a full-time business manager (*Geschäftsführer*) in every Kreisverband,[10] broadly in line with western staffing levels. The SPD is unable to maintain this level of professionalisation, with around 100 paid functionaries in the east, against around 950 in the west.[11] The relative organisational weakness of the all-German FDP means that it is unable to subsidise its eastern wing in the manner of the larger parties. The Brandenburg FDP has only seven paid officials (three of these seconded from Bonn), whilst the Sachsen-Anhalt party has only three. In Thüringen, the FDP adopted the imaginative expedient of deploying the state-financed personal assistants of Landtag deputies in party work, but, with the eclipse of the FDP in Landtag elections in 1994, this resource is no longer available.[12] The PDS dispensed with the vast bureaucratic apparatus of its predecessor through financial necessity following the relinquishment of SED assets to the Treuhand authority. It retains a professional staff of over 100 in its Berlin headquarters, with an equivalent number employed in the Länder.[13]

The electoral impact of local party organisation is difficult to assess authoritatively. Whilst some authors have downgraded the campaign effect of 'on the gound' party organisation, others have found a positive correlation between the size and activism of local party organisations and campaign intensity.[14] Author's interviews with party business managers in the new German Länder in 1994 suggested that with the exception of the

PDS all the parties had difficulty in mobilising members in the campaign, and that organisational weakness was widely perceived as an electoral handicap.

The Social Profile of Party Membership

The organic relationship between parties and society in western democracies is reflected in the social composition of the parties' membership and electorate. Although parties are now more amorphous in social composition than previously, most large parties continue to exhibit a recognisable social profile, and the image which a party projects via the social profile of its membership acts as a cue to voters. In the new German Länder, the social composition of party membership deviates quite significantly from that in the west.

The deviation is particularly striking in the two major parties (see Table 2). In the CDU, the self-employed are heavily underrepresented in comparison to the west, reflecting the weak development of the entrepreneurial middle class in the new Länder. Conversely, the proportion of manual workers is around three times higher than in the west. A quarter of CDU members are drawn from this social group in the new Länder, against one-tenth in the west. The most striking characteristic of the SPD in the east is the low level of manual worker membership, particularly in view of the larger size of the manual working class in the east. When the relative size of the two major parties is taken into account, the disparity is even more pronounced: the CDU contains around four times as many manual workers as the SPD. The dominant group in the SPD is white-collar workers, in particular the so-called 'technical intelligentsia' of engineers, teachers, health care professionals and scientists. In the Sachsen SPD these four professional groups represent fully 30 per cent of party membership.[15]

The social composition of FDP membership is broadly based and overlaps with that of the two major parties. Like the CDU it suffers from the small size of the entrepreneurial middle class: a strong area of recruitment in the west. Nevertheless it has a relatively high concentration of small entrepreneur tradesmen/craftsmen, a legacy of its block party roots. Like the SPD it also contains a concentration of the technical intelligentsia. In some areas like Sachsen-Anhalt, manual workers are quite heavily represented. The PDS is very heavily dominated by those outside the labour market: pensioners, the early retired and the unemployed. In the Sachsen-Anhalt party these elements make up 52 per cent, 12 per cent and 13 per cent respectively of party membership, over three-quarters of the total.

Ideological and Political Profiles

The political profiles of the parties in the new Länder are less clearly

TABLE 2

SOCIAL COMPOSITION OF PARTY MEMBERSHIP: CDU AND SPD %

	CDU Brndbg	CDU Sachsen	CDU West	SPD Sachs-An	SPD Sachsen	SPD FRG
Manual Worker	27.3	24.1	9.1	20	18	25.5
Clerical/ Managerial	36.1	32.2	28.7	41	42	26.6
High Grade Civil Servant	1.2	2.8	12.8	2	2	10.6
Self Emplyd	10.8	13.1	23.3	7	9	4.0
Student	1.8	3.4	3.6	1	4	6.6
Housewife	2.4	3.0	11.3	–	–	11.8
Pensioner	14.5	18.2	4.7	11	13	9.0
Unemployed	1.8	2.2	0.5	9	8	1.5
Other	4.2	1.0	5.9	9	4	4.4

Sources: CDU Brandenburg; CDU Sachsen: *Landesgeschäftsstellen;* SPD Sachsen; SPD Sachsen-Anhalt; *Landesgeschäftsstellen;* CDU Western Länder; Peter Haungs, 'Die CDU: Prototyp einer Volkspartei' in Alf Mintzel and Heinrich Oberreuter (eds.), *Parteien in der Bundesrepublik Deutschland,* (Opladen: Leske and Budrich, 1992), p.193; Gerhard Brauntal, The German Social Demorat Since 1969; *A Party in Power and Opposition,* (Boulder Col,: Westview Press, 1994), p.75.

defined than in the west. The mixed social composition of the parties operates against clear ideological positions. Moreover, ideological identities have not yet had time to crystalise. Ideological eclecticism is particularly marked in the CDU. Although initially espousing the western party's 'social market economy' leitmotif and advocating market-led reconstruction, the CDU in the east harbours a strong orientation towards state intervention.[16] However, whilst leaning towards the leftist tendency in Christian Democracy on economic issues, it displays more conservative inclinations on social issues. On the issue of political asylum, for instance, 82 per cent of CDU supporters in the east advocated tightening up the constitution, against 62 per cent in the CDU in the west and 72 per cent in the east overall. On the other hand, opinion on moral issues reflects the secular character of the CDU in the east. Only 24 per cent of party supporters support the criminalisation of abortion, against 42 per cent in the west.[17] Thus a tendency to the left on economic issues coexists with social conservatism, but liberal views on moral issues.

In the SPD it is possible to identify two broad cultural groupings: the founding group with a common background in the church and civil rights movements out of which the party emerged, and more recent recruits drawn from the technical intelligentsia. The commitment of the former to the principles of *Basisdemokratie*, and their liberal humanist value orientation conflicts with the more conservative-pragmatic perspectives of the technical intelligentsia.[18] It should be added, however, that the ideological cleavages characteristic of the SPD in the west (left/right, old politics/new politics) are much less clearly defined in the party in the east.

As in the west, the eastern FDP has an ill-defined ideological profile. Broadly identified as a 'middle class economics party' the eastern Landesverbände place greater emphasis on the social dimension. The tension between economic and social liberalism is thus exacerbated in the east. Bündnis 90/Die Grünen resembles the western Greens in their early years. Ideological heterogeneity in its membership and electorate makes it reluctant to commit itself to definite programmatic statements, preferring instead a 'programme of open concepts' (*Programmatik der offenen Konzepte*).[19] In contrast to the ideological homogeneity of its predecessor, the PDS membership and electorate is characterised by ideological diversity, reflected in party programmes. These combine an ill-defined 'socialist alternative' to the market economy with the 'softer' themes of the new left: ecology, gender issues, and participatory democracy.[20]

It can be concluded from the above that parties in the new Länder are characterised by an unusually low level of organisational intensity, reflected in a correspondingly low organisational capacity for electoral mobilisation. In terms of social composition, the parties deviate from their counterparts in the west, exhibiting markedly more social diversity. The classical linkages between parties and particular social groups are only weakly developed. The political profiles of the parties are less sharply defined than in the west, with all parties displaying sharp ideological diversity. In short, the party landscape in the new Länder is more open and fluid than in the west. It might therefore be expected that electoral relations would be characterised by a similar fluidity.

The Electoral Landscape

The Weakness of Socially Structured Partisanship

Despite a progressive weakening of the linkage between social structure and electoral behaviour in the old Federal Republic, significant sections of the electorate continue to vote along the line of class and religion. Socially structured partisanship provides the parties with a relatively stable core electorate, serving as a foundation of party system stability. In the new Länder, however, the Communist legacy of enforced social homogeneity produced what Offe has termed a 'social structure of repressed difference.'[21] Society lacks a sufficiently developed differentiation of socio-economic interests, status and cultural identity to generate stable patterns of group-based partisanship. Moreover, based on the post-industrial configuration of high technology specialist production, a diverse tertiary sector, and a flexible and polyvalent labour market, the inchoate market economy in the east is unconducive to western patterns of group partisanship rooted in the historic legacy of industrial society. A further source of stable partisanship is party identification – a psychological affinity between parties and voters. Survey data suggest that party identification is still weak in eastern Germany. Only 26 per cent express strong party ties and 37 per cent are without party attachments (respectively 35 per cent and 27 per cent in western Germany).[22] The experience of most western democracies suggests that party identification is subject to a long-term secular decline, unlikely to be reversed in a post-Communist society.

The evidence of the 1990 elections suggested that group-based partisanship played little part in structuring the electorate in the east. Indeed, the pattern of class voting was an inversion of expectations derived from the west. The centre-right parties won 61 per cent of the manual worker vote, (CDU 50 per cent: FDP 11 per cent) against 35 per cent for the parties of the left (SPD 25 per cent: PDS five per cent; Bündnis 90/Greens five per cent).[23] On the confessional dimension, the most striking characteristic is the very low level of religious affiliation.[24] Almost three quarters of the electorate lack even formal church ties (73 per cent secular: 24 per cent Protestant: three per cent Catholic). Whilst the overwhelming dominance of the CDU in both confessional groups suggests that church affiliation is a strong factor in partisanship, low levels of affiliation mean that religion is relatively insignificant in structuring the electorate overall.

Superwahljahr *in the New Länder*

In the absence of socially structured partisanship, issues play a major part in electoral choice in the east. In particular, voter choice is heavily influenced by perceptions of personal economic circumstances, the general state of the economy, and party competence at economic management. On all of these dimensions, critical movements of opinion occurred between early 1994 and the June to October period in which the elections took place. Trends were similar to those in the west, but were accentuated in the new Länder, with polls showing a steady increase in positive perceptions of personal economic circumstances. Favourable perceptions increased from 35 per cent to 42 per cent between February and September, whilst assessments of the the general state of the economy also became markedly more positive. On a scale of 'good'/'mixed'/'bad', the 'mixed' response increased from 43 per cent to 56 per cent whilst 'bad' fell from 54 per cent to 38 per cent. These positive trends were reflected in perceptions of party competence in economic management. In early 1994 almost 40 per cent expressed confidence in an SPD government, against barely 20 per cent for the CDU: by June the parties were even, and thereafter the CDU established a lead. Voting intentions for the two major parties followed a remarkably similar trend, with a double digit SPD lead transformed into a clear margin for the CDU.[25]

Sachsen-Anhalt was the first of the new Länder to hold Landtag elections, in June 1994, before the trend towards the CDU had consolidated. Moreover, local circumstances meant that this was the state most likely to experience a change of government. Firstly, with an economy based on machine building and chemicals, the state suffered particularly severely from the catastrophic structural decline of heavy industry in the east after 1990. Secondly, the CDU–FDP government in Sachsen-Anhalt had been the most unstable of all the new Länder, with a high incidence of scandals and internal conflicts, which had led to the resignation of two minister-presidents in four years. The first incumbent, Gerd Gies, stepped down after revelations that he had used Stasi allegations to manipulate Landtag candidate selection to his own advantage. His successor, Werner Munch, was forced to resign after the revelation that he and other ministers had helped themselves to inflated salaries. With this affair, CDU support was reduced to around ten per cent, and their ability to recover under the inexperienced and relatively unknown figure of new Minister-President Christoph Berger was questionable. In view of the circumstances, the Sachsen-Anhalt Landtag election was a boost to the CDU for forthcoming contests. Losing only 4.6 per cent of the vote, the CDU remained the largest party, albeit very marginally.

The result of the Sachsen-Anhalt election signalled two developments which carried far-reaching implications for the party system and coalition building, and which were to be replicated throughout the new Länder. The collapse of the FDP vote in what had been its eastern stronghold deprived the CDU of a centre-right coalition partner, and was indicative of a trend which was to sweep the Liberals from Land parliaments throughout the east. On the left, SPD gains were relatively modest, but the PDS virtually doubled its share of the vote, illustrating its potential as an east German interest/protest party. The new party configuration left only two coalition alternatives: a grand coalition of CDU and SPD, or a left majority government with some form of reliance on the PDS. Despite pre-election statements that there would be no deals with the ex-Communists, the SPD eschewed a grand coalition in favour of a left coalition with Bündnis 90/Die Grünen, with the tacit support of the PDS (Minister-President Reinhard Höppner was elected with the votes of the PDS). The political fallout from the Sachsen-Anhalt experiment was intense, figuring prominently in the Bundestag election campaign. Its implications for the structure of electoral competition and party system dynamics will be discussed below.

The Brandenburg and Sachsen Landtag elections held simultaneously in September 1994 displayed another facet of the electoral landscape in the east: the potential of personalities in an electorate where the bonds between parties and voters were weak. The personality factor was differently configured between the two Länder, and harnessed to different parties, but its effect was similar: an overwhelming single party majority in both states. In a number of ways, Brandenburg and Sachsen were mirror images of each other. Encompassing the east Berlin hinterland, Brandenburg housed large parts of GDR officialdom, and retained an identity with some aspects of the old regime, reinforced by its status as one of the poorest of the new Länder. It was the only state ruled by an SPD-led government after 1990, with the CDU organisationally and electorally impotent and torn by internal conflicts. Sachsen, on the other hand, rapidly forged a post-*Wende* regional identity. Although the state shared the east German experience of de-industrialisation, it had some success at attracting inward investment, and contained two centres of commercial potential: Leipzig and Dresden. In both Landtag and Bundestag elections in 1990, Sachsen emerged as the CDU's eastern stronghold. What the two states had in common, however, was a dominant minister-president with the status of *Landesvater*, in sharp contrast to the transient and rather colourless figures in the other eastern Länder.

Both elections were thus highly personalised. In Brandenburg, the easterner Manfred Stolpe was beleaguered by allegations of Stasi connections, orchestrated by the Bonn CDU, although echoed by some in his own ranks. Early in 1994 his SPD–FDP–Bündnis 90 government was deprived of a majority by defections from the ranks of his coalition partners. These pressures, however, merely served to activate Brandenburg's 'eastern reflex', strengthening bonds of personal loyalty between Stolpe and the electorate which extended well beyond SPD supporters. The ability of the prominent and charismatic westerner Kurt Biedenkopf to exercise a similarly broad personal appeal in Sachsen was based on overcoming, rather than personifying, cultural divisions between east and west. Assuming a second leadership role as Land party chairman in 1991, Biedenkopf's stature enabled him to defuse the threatening conflict between block party elements and 'renewers' which damaged the CDU in other eastern Länder.

His government also drew strength from the presence of nationally prominent easterners, Heinz Eggert and Steffen Heitmann. This unusual combination of circumstances produced remarkable results, with victories for Stolpe (54.1 per cent against 18.7 per cent for the CDU) and Biedenkopf (58.1 per cent against 16.6 per cent for the SPD). The divergence in electoral behaviour was unprecedented, with two adjacent Länder, voting on the same day, producing opposite party majorities on a massive scale. The impact of personalities was demonstrated by the unusually wide difference between party shares of first and second votes. In terms of first votes (direct votes for party candidates in electoral districts, and a measure of underlying partisanship), the CDU share in Sachsen was 50.4 per cent, some 7.1 per cent below its second vote share, whilst the 50.2 per cent SPD share of the first vote in Brandenburg was 3.9 per cent down on second votes. In each case the second vote bonus for the victor parties could be regarded as the minister-president bonus, leading INFAS to terms the poll 'presidential elections'.[26] This assessment was underlined by the Bundestag election when the CDU and SPD shares of the vote in Sachsen and Brandenburg 'normalised' at 48.0 per cent and 45.0 per cent respectively.

Landtag elections in Mecklenburg-Vorpommern and Thüringen were held simultaneously with the Bundestag election. The poorest of the new Länder, with the CDU–FDP coalition susceptible to scandal and personal rivalries, and discredited in mid-term by its insensitive handling of racist political violence in Rostock, Mecklenburg-Vorpommern appeared unpromising territory for the CDU. Minister-President Berndt Seite (successor to Alfred Gomolka, who had fallen victim to internal party intrigue in 1992), had only a marginal popularity lead over the SPD challenger. Moreover, the CDU trailed the SPD in voter perceptions of party competence.[27] The Christian Democrats' prospects in Thüringen appeared more favourable. The CDU–FDP government was also tainted by scandal, and had experienced a change of minister-president with the westerner Bernhard Vogel stepping in for Josef Duchac who lost the support of his Fraktion in 1992. Nevertheless, Vogel had a substantial popularity lead over his SPD rival, and his party had the advantage over the opposition in terms of voter perceptions of party competence.[28]

In both these states, the Christian Democratic vote held up relatively well, surprisingly better in Mecklenburg-Vorpommern (a mere 0.6 per cent down on 1992) than in Thüringen (2.8 per cent down). What saved the CDU from heavier losses was the coincidence of Landtag and Bundestag elections. With a turnout some 10–15 per cent, higher than earlier Land elections elsewhere in the east, the party was able to mobilise its supporters more effectively. SPD gains were relatively modest (2.5 per cent in

Mecklenburg-Vorpommern, 6.8 per cent in Thüringen), but as in Sachsen-Anhalt, the wipe-out of the FDP left only two alternatives: a grand coalition or SPD reliance on the support of the PDS. The relatively conservative Thüringen SPD quickly came to terms with the CDU for a grand coalition under Vogel. In Mecklenburg-Vorpommern, however, the SPD initially undertook a round of talks with the PDS, the first official dialogue of any sort between the two parties. SPD leader Harald Ringstoff subsequently dismissed this as tactical positioning for negotiation with the CDU over the grand coalition which finally emerged.[29] However, the SPD leadership in Bonn was greatly exercised, and the issue of relations with the PDS threatened to divide the all-German SPD.

Identifying Trends

Four main trends are evident from *Superwahljahr* in the eastern Länder. Firstly, and most prominently, a process of electoral concentration can be observed, with an increasing share of the vote going to 'core' parties, and the marginalisation of smaller parties. So pronounced is this tendency that the FDP was driven out of all five state parliaments, and Bündnis 90/Die Grünen survived in only one state. Amongst the 'core' parties, CDU losses were relatively limited, given the scale of economic decline under its governments in four of the Länder and in Bonn. Over the five states as a whole the party's share of the vote fell by only 0.9 per cent from 42.0 per cent to 41.1 per cent. The SPD share of the vote across the five Landtag elections increased modestly by 4.2 per cent from 25.8 per cent to 30.0 per cent. The real winner, however, was the PDS, with an increase of 5.5 per cent from 12.7 per cent to 18.2 per cent. Collectively, the core parties thus increased their share of the vote from 80.5 per cent to 89.3 per cent. These trends were mirrored in slightly magnified form in the Bundestag election.

A second striking feature of the Landtag elections is polarisation, with very significant gains for the PDS. In none of the Länder was the main opposition party able to make an effective challenge to the government. In Brandenburg and Sachsen, where, as has already been observed, governments were emphatically confirmed in power, the main opposition parties lost ground and the PDS came within a hairsbreadth of forcing them into third place. Only in Thüringen did the gains of the main opposition party exceed those of the PDS. This syndrome is indicative of a polarised electorate, to which the concept of moderate opposition is alien, and which either endorses the government, or expresses fundamental opposition.

The third conclusion which can be drawn from *Superwahljahr* in the east, is that the electorate is more volatile than that in the west. The application of the Pedersen Index (the sum total of gains and losses in party share of the vote, divided by two) to Landtag elections in all parts of

Germany between 1990 and 1994 shows an average index of electoral change of 14.8 in the east against 8.9 in the west.[30] Volatility is unsurprising given the above-mentioned weakness of socially structured partisanship in a new party system.

There is, however, evidence that patterns of partisanship in the new Länder may be normalising. A fourth tendency observable in 1994 was for class voting to move a little closer to that in the old Federal Republic. In the 1994 Bundestag election, support for the parties of the centre-right amongst manual workers fell from 60.8 per cent to 43.9 per cent,[31] only around five per cent higher than in the west, indicating that social groups may be gravitating to what would be regarded in the west as their natural political home (see Table 3). This development also provides an explanation for the catastrophic performance of the FDP, and for the rise of the PDS vote. The unusually high manual worker vote for the FDP in 1990 collapsed in 1994, whilst the PDS more than doubled its share of this section of the electorate.

TABLE 3

MANUAL WORKING CLASS VOTE BY PARTY –
BUNDESTAG ELECTIONS 1990; 1994 (%)

		CDU	SPD	FDP	GREENS	PDS
East	94	40.6	35.1	3.3	3.3	14.7
	90	49.8	24.8	11.0	5.0	5.3
West	94	35.0	49.5	3.6	5.2	1.1
	90	39.0	46.7	6.0	3.2	0.2

Sources: Forschungsgruppe Wahlen, Mannheim, Bundestagswahl 1990; eine Analyse der ersten gesamtdeutschen Bundestagswahl am 2 Dezember 1990, p.35; Forschungsgruppe Wahlen, Mennheim, Bundestagswahl 1994; eine Analyse der Wahl zum 13 Deutschen Bundestag am 16 Oktober 1994, p.22.

The Party System

The Foundations of the Post-1994 Party System

Party systems in western democracies are shaped by three sets of forces: the structure of social cleavages; the institutional parameters of the polity; and the structure of party competition. As has been observed above, the foundation of the system lies in the social structure. Stability is imparted by societal cleavages, defining social collectivities or milieux with distinctive cultural and political identities and interests, thereby structuring the electorate and ordering the party system. The stronger the cleavage structure, the more stable the party system. In the absence of cleavages, politics is individualised in an open electoral market in which party systems are correspondingly less stable. As has been observed above, the inchoate cleavage structures in the new German Länder are reflected in a looser systemic configuration, with some potential for instability and deviancy from western patterns.

Institutional parameters are influential at the secondary level of constraining party system formation. Certain electoral systems, for instance, restrict the proliferation of parties by erecting electoral hurdles, or by a system of relating representation to electoral strength which discriminates in favour of large parties. The institutional parameters of the new German Länder are, of course, those of the old Federal Republic, introduced by institutional transfer. In one important respect, however, they operate differently in the east. The *Bundeswahlgesetz* (Federal Electoral Law) makes provision for exemption from the five per cent hurdle for a party winning three 'direct mandates' (seats obtained by winning a majority of first votes for candidates in electoral districts). This circumstance had not occurred in the Federal Republic since the Deutsche Partei won 17 seats with just 3.4 per cent of the vote in 1957. The geographical concentration of the PDS vote, and its exceptionally high potential in east Berlin, however, enable it to take advantage of the 'direct mandate' provision. Combined with deviant social structures, this effect of federal electoral law contributes to the deviancy of the party system in the new Länder.

The third factor in party system formation reinforces deviancy in the east. Party competition in the western Länder is structured around the competitive axis between two dominant *Volksparteien*, perceived by the electorate as the principal parties of government and opposition. The western Länder have fallen into two categories: those in which the major parties alternate in Land government, and those in which one of the major parties exercises a permanent government role, with the weaker party cast in the opposition role. Grand coalitions have tended to be formed only in exceptional circumstances. Historically, the FDP has served a functional role as the pivot of a centre-oriented party system, and as a moderating coalition influence upon the major party of government. The Greens have exercised an agenda-setting role, maintaining the profile of new politics issues, and also a coalition role alongside the SPD.

The evidence of the 1994 elections suggests that party competition is structured differently in the new Länder. The *Volksparteien* are markedly less dominant, with the combined major party share of the vote hovering around 70 per cent as against a norm of around 80 per cent in the west. The opposition role operates differently: with their low electoral base in 1990 the opposition *Volkspartei* is unable to assert itself as credible challenger to incumbent governments. Moreover, opposition is perceived differently: 'fundamental' opposition, without aspirations to government, as represented by the PDS, has a stronger resonance, as against the 'moderate' and government-aspiring opposition of the out-of-power *Volkspartei*. In this polarised context, the functional role of the FDP is harder to sustain. Calculated coalition voting (splitting the first and second vote between the coalition partners) is rare. The FDP does not benefit as it does in the west from the bonus of second votes 'loaned' to it by supporters of the CDU. For Bündnis 90/Die Grünen, the low emphasis on new politics makes it difficult to play its agenda-setting role.

The Structure of Party Competition in a Polarised Party System

Landtag elections in the east in 1990 resulted in a party system which bore some resemblance to that in the west, both in terms of composition, and the positioning of the parties in relation to one another. The difference, of course, was the presence of the PDS, but its relatively small size meant that it remained an 'outsider', and the dynamics of the five-party system followed the four-party western model. With the consolidation of the PDS vote, and the eclipse of the FDP and (with the exception of Sachsen-Anhalt) Bündnis 90/Die Grünen, the post-1994 party system in the new Länder now deviates quite significantly from the western model. In many ways the PDS is now pivotal, in a polarised three-party system, the dynamics of which are significantly different from those of the more centre-oriented four-party sytem in the west. Whilst the party configuration in the western Länder provides the basis for a wide variety of coalition combinations, the alternatives in the east are very restricted. In the absence of the single party majorities which have emerged in Sachsen and Brandenburg, the only alternatives are a grand coalition as in Thüringen and Mecklenburg-Vorpommern, or a minority left coalition under the SPD, relying on the support of the PDS – the 'Sachsen-Anhalt experiment'.

Grand coalitions have been regarded as the last resort of government formation in the Federal Republic, since the overwhelming predominance of the two major parties unbalances the normal equilibrium of government and opposition. With the PDS as the third party, an over-powerful government is matched against a 'root and branch' opposition, distorting the equilibrium still further. The electoral response to this configuration of political forces is uncertain, but it is not unlikely that the PDS will benefit from the enhanced profile deriving from its role as the sole representative of opposition. On the other hand, the effect of the 'Sachsen-Anhalt experiment' may be to legitimise the PDS, consolidating its position in the party system.

This new political configuration creates strategic problems for the parties. The consolidation of the PDS faces the SPD with an especially sharp dilemma, between competition and co-operation with its rival on the left. With the left vote shared with the ex-Communists and Bündnis 90/Die Grünen, the SPD's chances of establishing dominance over the CDU (outside Brandenburg) are greatly reduced. A working relationship with the PDS, on the other hand, would yield rich opportunities for the formation of left coalitions in the new Länder. Co-operation with the PDS, however, is potentially damaging to the Social Democrats' electoral performance in the west, and would undermine the SPD's competitive strategy of portraying its rival as a 'superfluous irrelevance' in the party landscape. Unsurprisingly, the opportunity cost of co-operation is perceived differently between east and west. Whilst the SPD leadership in Bonn emphasises the dangers and urges a strict demarcation from the PDS, the party in the new Länder is much more open to co-operation. Accusing the Bonn leadership of responding 'hysterically', party leaders in the east advocate a more flexible strategy combining 'limited co-operation' with competition. The 'guidelines' issued in December 1994, precluding coalitions at both federal and Land levels, but allowing 'normal parliamentary contact',[32] were a compromise designed to grant the easterners some latitude within a broader framework of demarcation. It did little, however, to resolve the dilemma facing the party on the eastern fromt.

The increased prominence of the PDS in the new three-party system intensifies questions concerning its identity and function. As the sole representative of opposition in Thüringen and Mecklenburg-Vorpommern, equal opposition with the SPD and CDU in Sachsen and Brandenburg, and indispensable government prop in Sachsen-Anhalt, the PDS will have to tread a fine line between 'responsible' opposition and anti-system protest. The success of the PDS has been based on a formula of assimilation with liberal-capitalist society, combined with advocacy of an (ill-defined) socialist alternative to the market economy. The inherent inconsistency of this position (evident in its 1994 election programme) has been concealed beneath the emotional appeal of the PDS as a party of eastern interests. Its new prominence in the party landscape is likely to expose the conflict between anti-system tendencies in the PDS, and the left-liberal 'Realo' course which can already be detected in some sections of the party.[33]

The dilemma of the CDU is a tactical one. The 'demonisation' of PDS in the election campaign clearly failed to deter east Germans from supporting the party. Indeed, it was probably counterproductive, reinforcing the identification of easterners with 'their' party under attack from the west. The 'demonisation' campaign may thus have contributed to party system polarisation, with some negative effects for the CDU itself. On the other hand, for all the protestations of outrage at the presence of the PDS in the

Bundestag and Land parliaments in the east, the resultant division of the left is not inconvenient for the Christian Democrats. The costs and benefits, however, are difficult to balance, and the tactic may be a difficult one to sustain successfully in the longer term. The strategic dilemmas posed by the east–west split in the electoral and party landscapes are most intractable for the smaller parties. The FDP's role as economics party of the middle class (underlined by the campaign slogan 'the party of the better-off') is untenable in the east. A much stronger emphasis on social-liberalism is a prerequisite of recovery here. This is difficult to reconcile, however, with the predominance of economic liberalism in the federal party. For Bündnis 90/Die Grünen, the problem is to find a political niche. Much of the ground it stands on in the west (ecology, citizens rights, local issues) is occupied in the new Länder by the PDS.

Conclusion

The 1994 elections indicate that, four years after unification, the political landscape in the new German Länder is still significantly different from that in the west. Low membership, and a correspondingly limited capacity for 'on the ground' organisation, prejudices the ability of the mainstream parties to structure the electorate. Moreover, their amorphous social composition and weakly defined political profile means that voters do not receive the 'social cues' which help to structure partisanship in the west.

Weak partisanship is the most striking feature of the electoral landscape. Whilst this is partly a function of the structural weakness of the parties themselves, it reflects much more the weakness of socially structured partisanship characteristic of a post-Communist society in transition. Although group-based partisanship 'normalised' to some degree in 1994 (with the manual working-class shifting to the parties of the left), it remained weaker than in western Germany. Without a strong anchorage in traditional social milieux, electoral behaviour is more heavily influenced by fluctuations in economic circumstances, perceptions of party competence, and personalities.

Unsurprisingly, then, electoral volatility in Land elections between 1990 and 1994 was higher in the east than in the west. The east also experienced particularly pronounced variations in electoral trends between Länder, with elections on the same day in Brandenburg and Sachsen producing opposite party majorities on a massive scale. These two elections clearly showed that where partisanship is weak, personalities exercise an exaggerated influence in electoral choice. They also indicated the potential for electoral polaris-ation between the party of government, and the type of 'fundamental' opposition represented by the PDS.

Concentration and polarisation are the clearest tendencies emerging from the 1994 elections in the east, producing a less predictable and potentially less stable party system. The stabilising effect of the increase in the collective *Volkspartei* vote (SPD gains exceeded CDU losses) is outweighed by the polarising effect of the strengthening of the PDS, and the virtual wipe-out of the smaller parties. In a polarised three-party system, the PDS assumes a crucial role. Without the FDP and Bündnis 90/Die Grünen as coalition make-weights, and where there is no single party majority, government formation relies on either a grand coalition, or the support of the PDS (tacit or negotiated) for an SPD-led government. Both types of coalition bring together parties separated by some ideological distance. Moreover, government formation is more complex in a polarised three-party system. Mecklenburg-Vorpommern, for instance, saw a bizarre succession of post-election negotiations, with the SPD negotiating first with its ex-Communist opponent on the left, then (more successfully) with its Christian Democratic rival on the right.

Thus, the new structure of party competition in the eastern Länder, compounded by the party system split between east and west, makes very heavy demands upon the tactical dexterity of the parties. In short, the legacy of the 1994 elections in the new Länder is a more 'open political market' in which the capacity of the parties to structure and control politics is significantly reduced.

NOTES

The author wishes to acknowledge the support of the Nuffield Foundation for the research on which this article is based.

1. Peter Haungs, 'Die CDU: Prototyp einer Volkspartei', in Alf Mintzel and Heinrich Oberreuter (eds.), *Parteien in der Bundesrepublik Deutschland* (Opladen: Leske and Budrich, 1992), p.193; Clay Clemens, 'Disquiet on the Eastern Front; the Christian Democratic Union in Germany's New Länder', *German Politics* Vol.2, No.2 (August 1993), p.206.

2. Hans Vorländer, 'Die Freie Demokratischer Partei', in Mintzel and Oberreuter, *Parteien in der Bundesrepublik Deutschland*, pp.297–301; Christian Soe, 'Unity and Victory for the German Liberals', in Russell J. Dalton, *The New Germany Votes* (Providence and Oxford: Berg, 1993), pp.116–19.

3. *Germany Votes*, p.165; Thomas Ammer, 'Die Parteien in der DDR und in den neuen Bundesländern', in Mintzel and Oberreuter, *Parteien in der Bundesrepublik Deutschland*, p.455; Peter Joachim Lapp, *Das Zusammenwachsen des deutschen Parteiengefüges* (Bonn: Friedrich Ebert Stiftung, 1993), p.50.

4. Gerard Braunthal, *The German Social Democrats Since 1969; a Party in Power and Opposition* (Boulder Col.: Westview Press, 1994), pp.40–41; Ammer, 'Die Parteien in der DDR', p.472; Lapp, *Das Zusammenwachsen des deutschen Parteiengefüges*, p.31.

5. Thomas Poguntke and Rüdiger Schmitt-Beck, 'Still the Same with a New Name? Bündnis 90/Die Grünen after the Fusion', *German Politics*, Vol.3 No.1 (April 1994), p.98.

6. Piotr Sztompka, 'Civilisational Incompetence; The Trap of Post-Communist Societies',

Zeitschrift für Soziologie, Vol.22 No.2 (April 1993), pp.85–95.
7. Author's Interview, SPD Landesgeschäftsstelle, Sachsen; 15 Sept. 1994.
8. Author's Interview, FDP Landesgeschäftsstelle, Sachsen-Anhalt; 28 March 1994.
9. Author's Interview, PDS Landesgeschäftsstelle, Sachsen-Anhalt, 28 March 1994.
10. Author's Interviews, CDU Landesgeschäftsstelle, Brandenburg; 15 Sept. 1993; Sachsen-Anhalt, 29 March 1994; Sachsen, 14 Sept. 1994; Thüringen, 22 Sept. 1994.
11. Author's Interviews, SPD Landesgeschäftsstelle, Brandenburg; 14 Sept. 1993; Sachsen-Anhalt, 24 March 1994; Sachsen, 15 Sept. 1994; Thüringen 21 Sept. 1994.
12. Author's Interviews, FDP Landesgeschäftsstelle, Brandenburg, 16 Sept. 1993; Sachsen-Anhalt, 28 March 1994; Sachsen, 14 Sept. 1994; Thüringen, 22 Sept. 1994.
13. Author's Interviews, PDS Landesgeschäftsstelle, Brandenburg, 13 Sept. 1993; Sachsen-Anhalt, 28 March 1994; Sachsen, 16 Sept. 1994, Thüringen, 21 Sept. 1994.
14. Susan E Scarrow, 'Does Local Party Organisation Make a Difference? Political Parties and Local Government Elections in Germany', *German Politics*, Vol.2 No.3 (Dec. 1993), pp.377–92.
15. Author's Interviews, PDS Landesgeschäftsstelle, Brandenburg, 13 Sept. 1993; Sachsen-Anhalt, 28 March 1994, Sachsen, 16 Sept. 1994; Thüringen, 21 Sept. 1994.
16. Clemens, 'Disquiet on the Eastern Front', p.210.
17. Presse-und Informationsamt der Bundesregierung, *Zur politische Stimmung in Deutschland*, Nov.1992; Presse- und Informationsamt der Bundesregierung, *Zur politische Stimmung in Deutschland*, Jan. 1993.
18. Konrad Elmer, 'Vor - und Wirkungsgeschichte des Organisationsstatuts der SDP', in Dieter Dowe (ed.), *Von der Bürgerbewegung zur Partei; die Gründung der Sozialdemokratie in der DDR* (Bonn: Friedrich Ebert Stiftung, Reihe Gesprächskreis Geschichte, Heft 3, 1993), pp.29–39; Steffen Reiche, 'Motivationen der Gründergeneration', in Dowe (ed.), *Von der Bürgerbewegung zur Partei*, p.20; Stephen J. Silvia, "Loosely Coupled Anarchy; The Fragmentation of the Left', in Stephen A. Padgett (ed.), *Parties and Party Systems in the New Germany* (Aldershot: Gower, 1993), pp.171–89.
19. Jan Wielgohs, Marianne Schulz and Helmut Möller-Enbergs, *Bündnis 90. Entstehung, Entwicklung, Persecktiven; ein Beitrag zur Parteiforschung im vereinigten Deutschland* (Berlin: Berliner Debatte; Gesellschaft für sozialwissenschaftliche Forschung und Publizistik, 1992), pp.40–42.
20. Patrick Moreau, 'Die PDS; eine postkommunistische Partei', *Aus Politik und Zeitgeschichte*, B5/92, 24 Jan. 1992, pp.40–41.
21. Claus Offe, 'Capitalism by Democratic Design: Democratic Theory Facing the Triple Transition in East Central Europe', *Social Research*, Vol.58 No.4 (Winter 1991), pp.875–7.
22. Russell J Dalton, 'Two German Electorates?', in Gordon Smith, William E. Patterson, Peter Merkl and Stephen Padgett (eds.), *Developments in German Politics* (Basingstoke: Macmillan, 1992), p.71.
23. Forschungsgruppe Wahlen, Mannheim, *Bundestagswahl 1990; eine Analyse der ersten gesamtdeutschen Bundestagswahl am 2 Dezember 1990* (Mannheim: 1990), p.35.
24. Thomas Gauly, 'Konfessionalismus und politischer Kultur in Deutschland', *Aus Politik und Zeitgeschichte* B 20/91, 10 May 1991, p.45.
25. Press und Informationsamt der Bundesregierung, *Zur politische Stimmung in Deutschland*, March/April 1994; Press-und Informationsamt der Bundesregierung, *Zur politischen Stimmung in Deutschland*, Sept./Oct. 1994.
26. Frankfurter Rundschau, 13 Sept. 1994.
27. Forschungsgruppe Wahlen, Mannheim, *Wahl in Mecklenberg-Vorpommern; eine Analyse der Landtagswahl vom 16 Oktober 1994* (Mannheim: 1994), pp.26–9.
28. Forschungsgruppe Wahlen, Mannheim, *Wahl in Thüringen; eine Analyse der Landtagswahl vom 16 Oktober 1994* (Mannheim: 1994), p.33.
29. Handelsblatt, 25/26 Nov. 1994, p.9.
30. Author's calculations from Forschungsgruppe Wahlen, Mannheim, *Bundestagswahl 1994; eine Analyse der Wahl zum 13 deutschen Bundestag am 16 Oktober 1994* (Mannheim: 1994), p.A9.
31. Forschungsgruppe Wahlen, Mannheim, *Bundestagswahl 1994; eine Analyse der Wahl zum*

   13 deutschen Bundestag am 16 Oktober 1994 (Mannheim: 1994), p.22.
32. Frankfurter Rundschau, 7 Dez. 1994.
33. Wirtschaftswoche, 48, 24 Nov. 1994, p.27.

The *Enfant Terrible* of German Politics: The PDS Between GDR Nostalgia and Democratic Socialism[1]

JENS BASTIAN

The paper addresses three related questions about the most controversial political party represented in the Bundestag: the PDS. Who is this party? What is it? And where does it stand in the German party system? In highlighting the PDS' social profile, its internal debates about how to confront the legacy of the past and what its options are in the diverging political cultures of east and west Germany, it emerges that there is a future role for the PDS. However, the chances of consolidating its position depend as much on its own process of political clarification as on the tactics of the other parties. So far, the PDS has filled the gaps in the agenda left by the larger parties and successfully articulated the concerns of citizens in east Germany affected by the changes of unification. But without a broader base of appeal throughout the Bundesrepublik, the PDS faces an unpredictable future.

Introduction

The Party of Democratic Socialism (PDS), as the former Communists in the SED (*Sozialistische Einheitspartei Deutschland*) renamed[2] themselves after the Wall came down in 1989, was popping champagne corks when returning to the Bundestag in October 1994. But only a few months later, their January 1995 congress in Berlin mirrored a party which was caught in the midst of an identity crisis, desperately seeking to please everyone in the *Bunte Truppe* ('colourful team', the main PDS slogan for the parliamentary elections). For a number of reasons, which will be elaborated in detail below, it seems increasingly certain that the PDS will in some shape or form continue to play a role within German politics. The view which predominated in 1990 after the first post-unification elections that the PDS would enjoy only a short guest status in the Bundestag has proven unfounded.

The main political parties in Germany complain vigorously that the former SED, whilst responsible for the miserable condition of the east German economy is, through a simple change of name, now allowed to wear the mantle of respectability. While the CDU, SPD, Alliance 90/Greens and the FDP attempt in varying coalition types at the federal and Länder level to formulate feasible policies confronting the complexities of unification, and to sell these to an often disgruntled electorate, the PDS does not have such a need. By and large, they can sit on the sidelines, filling in the gaps and picking up the pieces where the main parties continue to fail or produce unwanted contradictions. The results of the election marathon in 1994 have shown, first and foremost in the eastern parts of Germany, that the PDS is unlikely to go quietly. For the time being, the other parties will, however reluctantly, have to learn to live with the PDS. To what degree such a learning process can include scenarios that see the PDS emerging as a coalition partner at the (east German) Länder level remains to be seen.

In what follows the paper will seek to address and answer three related questions: (i) What is the PDS? Here the focus is on the party's programme and ideological self-perception. Both features are part of the broader issue concerning how the PDS confronts the legacy of its past. Equally, while their catalogue of ideas may not add up to a coherent set of policies it is very effective in expressing radical populist opposition to the unification process. (ii) Who is the PDS? The social profile of the PDS is examined with regard to its members and voters. As will become apparent, there is an enormous difference between these groups. Finally, I will shed some light on the controversial search of the PDS for a (durable) position between the Alliance 90/Greens and the SPD in the German party system. The controversy over where the PDS should sit in the Bundestag, and subsequently who is her neighbour, reflects most distinctly this search.

What is the PDS?

No party in post-unification Germany is subject to such a diversity of, at times insulting, at other times revealing, labels than the PDS. What these labels have in common is the implicit assumption that the PDS is not a qualitatively new party but rather nothing more than a refurbished SED. To illustrate just a few classifications from the recent electoral campaign for the Bundestag: 'security association of former Stasi employees', 'league of veterans of the socialist GDR', or 'red-painted Fascists'. The latter label was used by the CDU in 1994, but the term was originally coined by the first post-World War II leader of the West German SPD, Kurt Schumacher. In doing so he emphatically rejected the forced unification of the SPD with the KPD to become the SED in East Germany. That the CDU would dig up the label almost 50 years later and use it against the PDS during the campaign was an exercise that alienated many citizens in east Germany, and insulted a number of PDS members who had a personal history of resistance against Nazi Germany. While such labels say relatively little about the PDS, a closer look at its programmatic profile proves vague to say the least. On a general level the PDS does not yet have a politically coherent programme for the whole of Germany. The new Länder constitute its political and programmatic theatre. By and large the demands and interpretations of the socio-economic situation in Germany are tailor-made for individual biographies and political identities of east German citizens. Such a bias is supplemented by a cocktail of programmatic features, which contributes to what one observer has labelled 'an imaginary museum of Socialism'. More specifically, if one were to understand the phenomenon PDS in light of its programme, and thereby arrive at identifying what is 'the left' in contemporary Germany, the endeavour would be rather confusing. In a word, the PDS is not yet a programmatic party with a coherent and comprehensive ideology.[3]

When scrutinising the January 1993 manifesto,[4] the second of its kind since 1990, a number of disquieting contrasts attract instant attention. On the one hand the PDS praises the 'world historic event of the Socialist October Revolution in 1917 [which] contributed to deeply positive developments for mankind in the 20th century'. Equally, a positive description of the establishment and consolidation of the GDR is still apparent in the programme. The PDS argues that 'justified anti-fascist and democratic changes in eastern Germany' motivated the state's creation. On the other hand the party sees its origins in the 'time of new departures during the Autumn of 1989 in the GDR'. With an eye to the winds of change sweeping through the streets of Leipzig, Dresden and East Berlin, the PDS stipulates that 'we wanted to contribute from within the SED to reform the GDR in an encompassing manner'. Finally, the disintegration of the former GDR is seen as the result of the 'incapacity to socialise the means of production in a feasible manner for the producers'. In other words, the demise of 'real existing socialism' in the GDR did not primarily originate through responsible actors and an ill-conceived political ideology. The former GDR and unified Germany are presented as political systems which both have deficits and contradictions. Such qualified interpretations and selective perceptions of the past by the PDS are deeply resented by the other parties, in particular the SPD and the Alliance 90/Greens. Both parties complain that the PDS is retroactively claiming credit for the Wall coming down while simultaneously expressing admiration for the events of 1917, and frequently erasing fundamental distinctions between a dictator-ship and liberal democracies through ill-conceived comparisons.

The PDS programme is much more explicit regarding the problems and challenges which the party claims to be fighting against than what it stands for in positive terms. The PDS is against (i) the 'westernisation' of the east, (ii) the 'dominance of capital', and (iii) the 'political system of the FRG'. By contrast, the party 'fights for parliamentary strength' but considers the 'outer-parliamentary struggle for societal change [as] decisive'. It wants to supplement parliamentary democracy with large elements of 'direct' democracy, in particular the inclusion of referendums and various citizen's councils, which are to be regularly consulted in the process of drafting legislation. In its economic section the programme argues for the introduction of the 30-hour week with full wage compensation. But with regard to property rights the details remain vague. It is not fully clear if property in general should be nationalised or just its availability. Such lack of clarity has an obvious background: the ideological legacy of property rights in the former GDR. While the political system has been abandoned, the notion that property should be more equally distributed remains prominent among large parts of the east German population; specifically, among those groups of citizens that have experienced or are being threatened with the loss of property in the painful process of restitution. The legacy of property rights and their perception within the population is a long-term argument working in favour of the PDS in the new Länder.

Who is the PDS?

A first answer to this question starts by analysing the string of electoral successes of the PDS during 1994. The recent Bundestag elections offer a promising initial avenue to explore. On a general scale the PDS gained in relative terms across east Germany, while in the west the strongest absolute increases in votes were attained in the city-states (*Stadtstaaten*) of Bremen and Hamburg. In the constituencies of east Berlin the PDS attracted 34.7 per cent of the total vote in the October 1994 parliamentary elections. In effect, the PDS became the *strongest* party in East Berlin. In relation to the whole of Berlin the PDS scored slightly under 15 per cent. The four single-member constituencies which it managed to win, and by means of which it therefore was able to avoid the five per cent threshold,[5] were all located in East Berlin. With regard to the five new Länder the PDS firmly established itself as the third strongest party, gaining almost 20 per cent, while in the west the score was 0.9 per cent! Furthermore, in both parts of Germany the voter configuration of the PDS is characterised by a distinct north–south slope. It does well in the former while struggling or stagnating in the latter.

When compared to the first Bundestag elections after unification in December 1990, the total number of PDS voters has changed very little over the past four years. All aspects considered, the results of the PDS in the

Superwahljahr 1994 point to a consolidation of the party's core voters. Compared with 1990, over four-fifths of the PDS voters remained faithful in the 1994 Bundestag elections. No other party in Germany can claim such a degree of commitment. In terms of electoral dynamics the reason for the PDS' persuasive showing is the decline of the other main parties in east Germany. This decline is most notably evident in the case of the CDU and the disintegration of the two smaller parties, the Alliance 90/Greens and the FDP.

Finally, lower voter participation in east Germany was also a positively contributing factor for the PDS results. Breaking the numbers down further into demographic characteristics, the PDS received over 20 per cent of the share of first-time voters in east Germany. This score was partly the result of the so-called *Bunte Truppe* (colourful team) which the PDS fielded as candidates for the elections: a mixed bag of former Communists, fellow-travellers, trade unionists and mavericks like the 81-year-old east German author, Stefan Heym, a personality with a record of opposition against the Honecker regime, but with an equally strong aversion to the western takeover of the former GDR.[6] How can we explain the overall success of the PDS, and, more specifically, was it surprising?

As a general point of departure emphasis has to be put on the fact that many east Germans feel their identity has been trampled on during the first five years of unification. This experience translated into a variety of predominantly emotional motives to support the PDS in the 1994 Bundestag elections. A sociological analysis of the reasons why so many men and women voted for the PDS reveals that a cocktail of subjective motives primarily shaped their decision-making processes. Vaguely defined positive memories of the former GDR, together with the feeling of having been put at a disadvantage socially by the association with west Germany, combine with the legacy of socialist values. In other words, the aspirations of PDS voters are a 'mixture of ideology, nostalgia and protest'.[7] The consequences of the breakdown of the old stability in the GDR are regarded by many people, particularly of the 18–25 and 50–65 years generations, as nothing short of a catastrophe. Furthermore, the preference for the PDS corresponds with educational status. The higher the level of education, the greater the propensity to vote for the PDS.

This observation also implies that the PDS is *not* the preferred party of blue-collar workers, the unemployed, or those working in agriculture, nor is the party strongly supported by the *Vereinigungsverlierer* (losers from unification). Differentiated according to income, education, urban residence and status, the PDS voters were formerly part of the privileged class in the old system. Many party workers, employees in the service sector and state functionaries found security and predictability in the old system as opposed to the uncertainties and turbulent environment of the new emerging economic order. Unable to adjust rapidly to the sweeping winds of change, and frequently alienated by the arrogance of the *Wessis*, many search for institutional stability and means to compensate for the loss of prestige with regard to their west German neighbours. The PDS is such a means of compensation, offering emotional attachment to those feeling excluded and expressing some of the values and traditions of the old system.

This strong cultural component is matched by an organisational structure and members' commitment which enables the PDS to offer different services and kick-start various political initiatives outside electoral campaigns. Cultural programmes, political discussion evenings, local and neighbourhood initiatives, information material, advice and assistance in bread-and-butter issues such as pension rights and rent problems make the PDS not only appear active and concerned, but above all present, fast to react to grievances and with an ear to the population's aspirations. No other party in east Germany manifests such political mobilisation capacities. This combination greatly contributes to the establishment and subsequent reinforcement of intellectual and emotional affiliation, an experience of togetherness paired with professional attitudes in everyday-life problems shared by many voters and sympathisers of the PDS.

The PDS' east German identity is, so far, its strongest card. Ironically, although the SED undertook numerous efforts, it never succeeded in creating an east German identity during the 40 years of the existence of the GDR. But after only four years of unified Germany, the frequent and obvious use of the term 'identity' in relation to citizens of the new Länder is particularly noteworthy. The sense of defending *Ossis'* interests is reinforced by the behaviour of the two major parties in Bonn. Both the west German Christian and Social Democrats talk of, and the former even treats, the PDS as a totalitarian danger.

But the tactic of demonising the PDS backfired in the electoral campaign for the Bundestag. Many east Germans expressed their willingness to vote for the PDS, not because they agreed with their politics, but because they believed that the party was being unfairly treated. In that respect, the views express a perception amongst east Germans regarding the ignorant and rejective attitude of the *Wessis* for the complexities of the former GDR. This includes a distinct hypocrisy in the controversies over the PDS. Many east Germans argue that the former *Blockflöten* party members[8] were readily welcomed as new and credible members within the CDU and the FDP, while PDS members are not credited with the ability to change. Double standards such as these link with the notion amongst many east Germans that the main parties from the west expect them to be grateful for the benefits of unification, and therefore vote without reservations for the CDU,

FDP or SPD. In other, slightly polemical, words, this expectation amounts to always saying grace for unification before having dinner in the east.

Turning from electoral success to party organisation, how does the PDS membership compare with its voters? First and foremost it must be underlined that 90 per cent of the currently 128,000 members were former SED members. This fact constitutes a structural impediment to openly and wholeheartedly confronting the SED legacy within the PDS. In doing so, the PDS leadership must always bear in mind that alienating major segments of its membership is a risk-prone endeavour. In the western parts of Germany the PDS claims to have slightly over 1,400 members. Compared to 1989 the total membership of the PDS has dramatically declined. On the eve of its 40th aniversary, and a month before the Berlin Wall fell, the SED claimed 2.3 million members, equivalent to 16 per cent of the GDR population.

A paradox in the present PDS membership development is the fact that it is continuously losing members, and thus organisational representation capacity in towns and villages. The example of Brandenburg is illustrative. In 1990 the PDS had 150,000 members. Four years later that figure had dropped to 18,258. But at the same time the party manages to receive up to 40 per cent of the vote in municipalities, for instance in Potsdam and Neu-Brandenburg. If we compare the PDS with the SPD then the difference in present membership is striking and further explains the former's organisational resources. The Social Democrats have roughly 26,000 members in the east, while the PDS has four times more! More specifically, in a constituency like Berlin-Lichtenberg the PDS can mobilise 4,800 members and the SPD can match this number with only 300. Such enormous differences shed further light on the PDS' performance in terms of presence, activities, initiatives, mail-box distributions and so on.

Contrary to popular assumptions the PDS membership configuration does not make the organisation a working-class party. The majority of its members are white-collar employees and academics, in gender terms overly male and with regard to age cohorts dominated by pensioners. In a word, the PDS is predominantly a party of the elderly. According to its own statistics two-thirds of the membership are pensioners or list their status as being in early retirement. Only five per cent of the total membership are young people up to the age of 30. Such an enormous diversity and imbalance places the PDS in a highly ambiguous position: how can the party keep the 'old(er) comrades' happy, with their political identity being subject to considerable challenges after having 'lost the GDR' on the one side, while avoiding the stigmatisation of being a symbol of the past, characterised by nostalgia and lack of adaptability towards the younger voters[9] on the other hand. The sociological category of 'relative deprivation' further helps to clarify the picture. Amongst many members the opinion is voiced that they have experienced a decline in status since 1990, a decline which is less obvious in terms of disposable income, but more in sinking prestige in society. Such experiences feed into a culture of resentment among the population against the 'self-proclaimed winners of history' (party programme). The PDS readily exploits these perceptions together with the manifest frustrations of those whose high expectations have been greatly disappointed in the course of the past five years.

The party leader, Lothar Bisky, a former film academy rector, expressed the diversity and fragmentation within the PDS as follows: 'I come from a party which was always right, and I am now in a party, which consists of ten parties, all of which are right'.[10] While the fourth party congress in January 1995 declared Stalinist positions as incompatible with membership within the PDS, it refused to draw the line with members of the so-called 'Kommunistische Plattform'. The leading representative of the hardline Platform is Ms Sahra Wagenknecht, 25 years old, member of the national executive and the party's *enfant terrible* with a penchant for GDR nostalgia.[11] Five years after the events of November 1989 orthodox members like Ms Wagenknecht readily claim that the former GDR was the first attempt on German soil to live without capitalists and profit mechanisms. According to the purists from the Communist Platform, who total approximately 5,000 members and are disproportionately influential as well as vocal in the party,[12] the decline of socialism began at the historical XX party congress of the Soviet CP in 1956 when N. Chruschtschow condemned Stalin's crimes. Such statements, notwithstanding their historical inaccuracy, are frequently taken as evidence by the other political parties that the PDS' internal reform process is only implemented on the surface and not in substance. By the same token, the PDS maintains that it refuses to commit itself to the *avant-garde* model of a socialist cadre party, but it is not prepared to disentangle itself fully from the October Revolution and its Leninist methods. Other historical controversies focus on the PDS' unbroken admiration for the Communist Party (KPD) during the Weimar Republic. In other words, much is still possible and acceptable within the PDS, partly originating from the legacy of the past and the sequencing of organisational transition, partly as a result of a calculated lack of political clarity.

For some, however, this deliberate vagueness is proof of avoiding a clear confrontation with the party's past. As a result they vote with their feet. Ms Karin Dörre, a member of the PDS national executive, resigned in advance of the 1995 party congress, citing irreconcilable differences. Ms Dörre claimed that the PDS is not sufficiently willing to confront its past in programmatic terms nor with regard to personnel policies, in particular the interaction between the SED and the secret police (*Stasi*). Compared to three years ago, when the PDS undertook a fresh start, the tide had changed. Solidarity was now more readily being expressed within party ranks for the former GDR élites than with those men and women who were on the side of political opposition in 1989.

As evidence for such an assertion two recent cases are instructive. On the one hand the rise of André Brie within the PDS: although he failed to declare voluntarily on earlier occasions his decade-long past as a Stasi informer, he narrowly failed to become the party operations manager after having organised the campaign of the PDS in the 1994 parliamentary elections. On the other hand, after the Bundestag elections the female MP Kaiser-Nicht was pressured to resign her seat because of serving as a Stasi informer on foreign students during the seventies in Leningrad. What looked like an attempt to clean house was in fact an embarrassing act of political manoeuvring within the PDS. Evidence of her former activities had repeatedly surfaced during the campaign, but Mrs Kaiser-Nicht (supported by the party leadership) emphatically refused to withdraw from the race. In short, some inside, and many outside, the PDS now see a former Stasi career as a recommendation, and not necessarily a hindrance for climbing the party ladder.

The PDS in Search of a Place Between the SPD and Alliance 90/Greens

From the outset the PDS, which was initially termed SED/PDS during the turbulent events of November–December 1989, faced a major challenge with regard to its name and position. Because the east German Social Democratic Party (SDP, later merging with the west German SPD) was secretly created in October 1989, the SED/PDS could not follow the trajectory of the Hungarian or Polish Communist parties, both of which dissolved themselves, with a radical communist faction remaining committed to the principles of orthodoxy. The newly established parties in both countries saw themselves as based on social democratic objectives. By contrast, this political terrain was occupied by the SDP, thus forcing any other leftist party to redefine its position in the emerging organisational landscape of the GDR in late 1989 and early 1990. The complete dissolution of the SED/PDS was briefly considered by the leadership but then rejected, not least because by ensuring legal continuity the PDS would be able to inherit large assets of the SED.

Next to historical considerations, the international perspective is instructive for another reason. Compared with the electoral success of former Communist parties in neighbouring countries, the results of the PDS are rather modest but in line with the general trend. In Poland, the reformed Social Democratic Alliance (SLD) is in a coalition government with the

PSL (Peasant Party), in Budapest the renamed Hungarian Socialist Party (MZsP) has an absolute majority in parliament and is engaged in a coalition with the Free Democrats (SDsZ). In both countries, the process of social democratisation of former Communist parties is in full swing, with pragmatic politics being the order of the day. Finally, in Bulgaria the former Communists, now termed Bulgarian Socialist Party (BSP), won an absolute majority of seats in the December 1994 elections. Hence, five years after the demise of communism, the impression is hardly avoidable that former Communists seem to be back everywhere one looks. Still, placed in the comparative context of post-communist politics, the major difference to date between the Polish and Hungarian former Communist parties and the PDS is the following: the latter knows that it will not be forced for the time being to prove its capacities and commitment to change by assuming governmental responsibility.

The problems of privatising the economy together with the high expectations of the citizens is one of the root causes for the return of many different ex-communist parties to power in central and eastern Europe. For the PDS the same applies, but it has not yet succeeded in gaining seats in any Länder government. But in the view of many it is close in doing so; for some even, the PDS has already managed to achieve this objective. The case of Sachsen-Anhalt, where a minority government of SPD and Alliance 90/Greens took office in the Summer of 1994, is seen as the first diplomatic recognition of the PDS in the political power game. For conservative critics the Rubicon has been crossed. While the PDS is not sitting at the government table, her presence in the room next door is critical for the attainment of parliamentary majorities.

Termed the 'Magdeburger Sündenfall',[13] both the CDU and FDP argue that the danger is growing that the indirect influence of the PDS on the decision-making process of the coalition establishes itself as a routine pattern. That such a view is not only the result of disgruntled CDU/FDP MPs, who now have to sit on the hard opposition benches in Sachsen-Anhalt, was illustrated by the resignation of the state's economics minister, J. Gramke, in November 1994, after only 100 days in office. The SPD member complained that more and more government decisions were based on showing consideration for the PDS' positions. Still, the reactions to the experiment in Magdeburg reflect the diverging political cultures in Germany. Although seen with a degree of scepticism, many in the east do not share the emphatic rejection of the experiment amongst western politicians, in particular those in the CDU and FDP. While many in the east see with reservation the fact that the PDS is becoming a pivotal actor in an emerging three party system in the new Länder, they do not reject outright the possibility of coalition combinations which include the PDS. What is most important for those concerned in party politics in the east is the necessity to have an open discussion about the possible scenarios. In that context the manner in which the Magdeburg experiment was presented took many by surprise. The SPD failed to initiate an internal debate about the eventuality of such a political constellation.

If the SPD is to achieve its dual political objective against the PDS, that is rejection of any form of collaboration above the local level whilst attracting PDS voters, then the Social Democrats must present a highly diversified profile which incorporates very different political cultures and programmatic ideas. With regard to earlier attempts to achieve this enormous goal, namely the integration of the Green electorate during the eighties, the outcome is rather clear: it widely failed, and the latter party is increasingly being recognised as a small *Volkspartei*, firmly established in the German party system and more and more courted by CDU representatives seeking new majorities in the future.

The SPD cannot avoid confronting the challenge of the PDS. In the process of this confrontation party positions have to be clarified regarding the definition of a democratic left in unified Germany. The strategy of the PDS is focused on the same challenge, but from a very different point of ideological departure. To a considerable degree it has managed to monopolise the term 'democratic socialism' and present itself as the voice of the east. What the SPD cannot afford to let happen is that the PDS presents itself as the leftist version of Social Democrats, the latter being portrayed as out of touch with the aspirations of men and women in east Germany. In that context, SPD representatives in the new Länder have repeatedly expressed irritation at the way the party leadership in Bonn has tried to sanction or discipline those in the east who express diverging forms of confronting the PDS. A major issue in the aforementioned clarification process concerns the PDS' interpretation of the merger of the SPD and KPD to form the SED in 1946 in the former GDR. To date, the PDS refuses to employ the term *Zwangsvereinigung* (forced unification). But it has recently acknowledged in a party declaration that SPD members were 'subject to considerable and unjustifiable pressure' during and after the parties' merger.[14]

With regard to the Alliance 90/Greens, in the course of the past four years the PDS has managed to replace the Bündnisgrüne as the party of eastern protest. Its definition of contemporary dissidence allows the PDS to present itself as the only real party of opposition, while the initiators of the peaceful revolution of 1989 are now politically marginalised, seen as being out of touch with the electorate and reminiscing about the recent past. It must be of great concern for the Greens in east and west, and a considerable disillusionment for many former dissidents, who took enormous personal risks in their struggle for civil rights during the eighties in East Germany, to see that the PDS has successfully managed to be regarded as a party of protest with an electable leadership. Essentially a west German party, it is becoming increasingly difficult to convincingly identify what the Alliance 90/Greens stand for in east Germany.[15] With appeal to socio-cultural milieus and groups, who in the eighties would have been primarily addressed by the Greens, and to a lesser extent the SPD, the PDS succeeded in gaining considerable support from the Green voter reservoir. The results of the 1994 Bundestag elections in Berlin are a striking example. The relationship of the PDS to the Greens is defined by the former as one of competition, but as with the SPD, both parties are not regarded as the political enemy. A motion, accepted during the recent Berlin congress, argues that a working relationship must 'gradually' be established with such 'competitors' inside and outside parliaments.

The breaking away of the social base of the Alliance 90/Greens in the new Länder, and their replacement by the PDS and the SPD, fundamentally changes the rules of the political game in east Germany. Compared to four years ago, the Social Democrats have made steady progress and are now in four of the five governments in the new Länder. However, in two of these states, Thüringen and Mecklenburg Vorpommern, the SPD has formed so-called 'grand coalitions' with the declining CDU, and the PDS is the sole representative of opposition in both regional parliaments. From the CDU's perspective, the primary objective of these coalitions is to prevent the rising PDS from attaining political power in regional parliaments. For its part, the SPD is caught in a dilemma: while it is increasing its share of the vote and the Alliance 90/Greens are voted out of the regional parliaments, the SPD is virtually left with no alternative other than to form a coalition with the CDU. In other words, the Christian Democrats can regularly put pressure on the SPD's strategic decisions because the only remaining feasible option is a SPD/PDS coalition.

Conclusions

The electoral success of the PDS at the regional and federal levels during 1994 is as much an impressive achievement as it is its greatest legacy. The success has brought, and will continue to bring, to the fore internal conflicts about the future course and priorities of the party. These internal contradictions were simmering but successfully contained by the role which the party played in the 1994 election marathon: 'to advance change through opposition' as its central slogan stated. Now the debate is open concerning how to define such change, and if the means of opposition are the most convenient political tools to focus on. But the çore challenge to the PDS, which will determine its future chances in the west German electorate, is the need to draw a clear chalk line with the past. The scope and content of the PDS' examination of the SED dictatorship is the determining element in the party's ideological profile.[16] The January 1995 congress sought to provide much needed clarification, but even the party leader, Bisky, acknowledged that the PDS is 'still searching' and there continues to be 'resistance' within the rank-and-file.[17] While it is willing to criticise, within limits, 'degenerations' of its legal predecessor, the SED, the PDS cannot go too far too fast without risking offending large sections of its membership. The PDS has shown itself above all to be a party of the milieu, a party specific to its social environment and culture. Yet at the same time it represents a solid constituency and has proved itself expert in tackling issues of local concern, which has enabled it to consolidate its powerbase in eastern Germany, accumulating between 15 and 45 per cent of the vote in some regions of the former GDR. While, in the east, even the party's opponents have reluctantly acknowledged that it is too early to write the PDS off, the future of the organisation is ultimately decided in the west. But there the stigmatisation of being the SED epigone remains a sticky issue. Furthermore, how two political cultures can be brought under one umbrella, big enough to accommodate those fringes of the west German left outside the SPD and the Greens as well as hard-core Communists with east German political identities, could turn out to be as taxing as squaring the circle. Any visit to party meetings in Berlin are illustrative of this challenge. The visitor is unexpectedly reminded of the political culture of the late seventies in West Germany where sectarian and esoteric disputes were its trade mark. Trotzkyists, Spartakists, Stalinists, Communists, Anarchists and Maoists are present, further supported by veterans of the squatter movement. This blend of the leftist past discusses with former SED members the perspectives of socialism in a party which has only existed for five years, and has hardly any social base outside the five new Länder. The Greens in West Germany needed almost 15 years to clarify these perspectives. The PDS will not be awarded the luxury of so much time.

The Länder elections in Bremen in May 1995 have been singled out by the PDS as the first hurdle to test their standing in the west after the Bundestag ballot. With the help of the financial and personnel resources of the eastern sections of the PDS the party is seeking to clear the five per cent threshold. Such support is necessary because the PDS in Bremen only has 52 members. By introducing open lists the party hoped to attract non-members as candidates for parliament. During the parliamentary elections in October 1994, the PDS received 2.95 per cent in Bremen. For that purpose, the *Go West* strategy of the PDS is to be achieved by primarily recruiting amongst disillusioned former SPD and Alliance 90/Greens voters, who see both parties, albeit for different reasons, as having dropped their radical appeal.

The party leadership knows that without a broader base of appeal throughout the Bundesrepublik, the PDS faces an unpredictable future. The legacy of the past, and even more so the internal contradictions of the party may yet prove its death knell. Equally, attracting votes from those disillusioned with German unification cannot remain the central reason for supporting the PDS. For the past five years the success of the party has largely been defined by the failure of the other parties to come up with coherent solutions for economic, social and cultural problems of unification. However, this may not always benefit the PDS and cannot be in its long-term interest. By the same token, the political survival of the PDS is influenced by the capacity to overcome the image of being a regional party voicing eastern protest. Even if the federal structure of the German political system benefits the PDS, a second version of the Bavarian CSU, in the form of a *Lega East*, would run counter to the objective of the party leadership, namely to establish itself as the only effective left-wing opposition party in Germany.

The PDS must therefore decide how it wants to establish itself as a stable organisation with democratic principles, structures and objectives. Any achievements in these areas will open the door for the PDS to become a viable actor in the highly dynamic coalition arithmetics of contemporary German politics. Yet, let there be no doubts: the controversies surrounding the PDS can only be fruitful if they reach the citizens in east Germany. By contrast, the conflicts with such an *enfant terrible* risk being devastating for the political culture in Germany if they are characterised by west German behaviour of domination and arrogance, instrumentalising such debates for power struggles in Bonn. In that context the PDS challenge is part of a much wider problem in post-unification Germany: that the anxieties and preoccupations of the west dictate the political constellations in the east.

Whether the party will outlive its own problems remains to be seen. A telling indicator for the possibility was illustrated in January 1995. The anniversary of the death of the murdered German Communist heroes Rosa Luxemburg and Karl Liebknecht was commemorated at the site where they were murdered: the *Landwehr* canal in Berlin. In the years of the GDR crowds of 100,000 organised demonstrators would march in East Berlin under the watchful eyes of the SED authorities and Stasi police. By contrast, in January 1995, with no coercion to attend, the PDS organised with other political groupings a commemoration march which attracted over 80,000 people! Amongst the marchers, many were too young to be blamed for the demise of the GDR, and others expressed their origin as being from the western part of Germany.

NOTES

1. I am grateful to Torun Dewan, Calliope Spanou and Willie Paterson for helpful comments on an earlier version.
2. More precisely, the SED renamed itself the PDS in February 1990 at an extraordinary party congress.
3. Patrick Moreau, Jochen Lang and Viola Neu, *Was will die PDS?* (Frankfurt a.M.: Ullstein Verlag, 1994).
4. See 'Programm der Partei des Demokratischen Sozialismus', *Disput*, Pressedienst PDS, Sonderheft, Feb. 1993.
5. The 4.4 per cent which the PDS received overall in the Bundestag elections translated into 30 seats. Five MdBs are from the west. The result implied that the PDS doubled its share of the vote compared with 1990. In fulfilling the condition of gaining more than three parliamentary constituencies outright (under the first of two votes cast in the German electoral system) the PDS was able to return to the Bundestag. The fact that these seats were all won in east Berlin lets the regional elections in the capital city, which are to be held in October 1995, assume further importance and controversy.
6. Stefan Heym won his seat in the constituency of central Berlin, narrowly outdistancing Wolfgang Thierse, the east German deputy party leader of the SPD. The Social Democrats had tried in vain to persuade the Christian Democrats in that constituency to support the SPD candidate in order to avoid the PDS gaining one of the three needed seats for circumventing the five per cent threshold. Since Heym is the oldest elected member of the Bundestag, he had the honour of opening the first session of parliament, thereby giving the PDS a formidable public relations success. His speech reflected widespread anger at the contradictions of unification, mixed with passionate demands for consensus politics. The conservatives refused to pay respect to Heym by remaining seated in the Bundestag when he started his speech. In the words of one commentator, Heym 'is well on his way to become the Hindenburg of the German left'.
7. Jürgen W. Falter and Markus Klein, 'Die Wähler der PDS bei der Bundestagswahl 1994. Zwischen Ideologie, Nostalgie und Protest', *Aus Politik und Zeitgeschichte*, 51-52/94, 23 Dec. 1994, pp.22–34.
8. The Blockflöten parties included the CDU and the LDPD (the East German liberal party), both closely tied to the SED and serving as transmission belts under the guise of formal independence. Their members and resources (organisational as well as financial, in particular property) were incorporated into the west CDU and FDP respectively without any major ideological difficulties.
9. The popularity of Gregor Gysi with his John Lennon-type glasses is one of the major assets of the PDS which attract younger voters and members. Equally, the election of a 23 year old woman, Angela Marquardt, as deputy party leader during the January 1995 congress, signals increased emphasis within the PDS leadership on its image towards younger people.
10. *Frankfurter Allgemeine Zeitung*, 20 Feb. 1995.
11. Shortly before the congress, Ms Wagenknecht called the quashing of the 1968 Prague Spring 'the suppression of the counter-revolution'. Bisky responded by saying that he 'feels shivers running down my back' at Ms Wagenknecht's remarks. The Plattform is subject to surveillance by the constitutional protection agency (*Verfassungsschutz*). Ms Wagenknecht lost her seat on the 18-member national executive during the January 1995 congress.
12. Ann L. Phillips, 'Socialism with a New Face? The PDS in Search of Reform', *East European Politics and Societies*, Vol.8, No.3 (Fall 1994), pp.495–530.
13. Magdeburg is the capital city of Sachsen-Anhalt. The term is best translated as: 'reprehensible act'. See Thomas Falkner and Dieter Huber, *Aufschwung PDS. Rote Socken - zurück zur Macht?* (Munich: Knaur Verlag, 1994).
14. See the declaration of the PDS in Mecklenburg-Vorpommern regarding its relation to the SPD: 'Auch Kommunisten können Demokraten sein', Nov. 1994.
15. This difficulty is reinforced when looking at the configuration of MdBs. Of the 49 MdBs in the Bundestag only five are from the new Länder.
16. Manfred Gerner, *Partei ohne Zukunft? Von der SED zur PDS* (Munich: Tilsner Verlag, 1994).

17. Lorenz Maroldt, 'Wie man künftig demokratisch sein will. 4. Parteitag der PDS in Berlin', *Das Parlament*, 3 Feb.1995.

Politikverdrossenheit and the Non-Voter

MICHAEL EILFORT

The attention paid to Politikverdrossenheit necessitates a careful analysis of the phenomenon of non-voting and the reasons for it. The abstentionist trend continued in Superwahljahr, though the implications of this for democracy are debatable. Certainly there is no 'party of non-voters': abstentionism is caused by many different factors. In addition to non-voting which is a fiction (caused by electoral arrangements) and involuntary non-voting, social isolation and the decline in feelings of civic obligation to vote are important causes. A new type of 'selective' non-voting is also on the increase, and it is this that is associated with rejection of parties, by voters who are often politically well-informed. Anyway, levels of abstention in Germany can be considered to be now reaching the 'normal' levels of other western democracies.

The Abstentionist Trend Continues

With the election of the 13th Bundestag on 16 October 1994 came the conclusion of *Superwahljahr* ('Super-election year') which, with more than 20 opportunities to cast a vote at the federal, Land, local council and European levels, had bestowed upon Germany a unique profusion of election dates. At the start of this election year the – for many people, worrying – question was posed: how would the real or supposed *Politikverdrossenheit*[1] of many Germans (often discussed in 1992 and 1993) take effect? Would the tendency of citizens towards electoral abstention and protest voting continue to increase, because people, as a result of opinion poll results and views expressed in the mass media, had an increasingly negative image of politicians as self-serving and elitist and as either too quarrelsome or insufficiently profiled, were frustrated by the lack of genuine alternatives to choose between at elections and the lack of opportunity to play a role in politics, and were angered at the deficiency of solutions to 'real' problems?

On the evening of 16 October 1994, when once again, as on almost every election night, every party wanted to be seen as the electoral victor, the established parties seemed to agree on one thing at least: the winner in

Superwahljahr was, above all, democracy itself, according to initial assessments. By the time the Bundestag election results were known, if not earlier, it was evident that in particular the increasing tendency of Germans to abstain from voting had been halted and that the political system had been thereby strengthened.

Such conclusions might be pleasant to hear, but are based upon false suppositions and premature assessments. It would anyway be miraculous if the non-voting section of the populace, which, at the zenith of the period of *Politikverdrossenheit*, had been graced with the epithet of a democracy-threatening 'party of abstainers', should now practically as a favour have dissolved itself.

The facts are as follows. Participation in the Bundestag election rose in comparison to 1990 by 1.3 per cent. In western Germany it increased by about two per cent; in eastern Germany it declined by about two per cent. In formal terms, then, the trend over many years towards increasing abstentionism seems to have been terminated. But what is the significance of such a small increase in turnout in an election whose outcome, in contrast to that of 1990, was exceptionally uncertain; in the course of which, again in contrast to 1990, a polarisation developed which stimulated mobilisation of the electorate; and in which appeals for electoral participation were made on a scale never before encountered?

It is also true that in the European Parliament election, for which comparative data from 1989 are only available for the western Länder, turnout declined markedly (with the exception of Baden-Württemberg, where elections to local councils took place simultaneously). The same applies to all the Länder elections in 1994 – with the exception of Bayern – other than those occurring on the same day as the Bundestag election. In Sachsen-Anhalt, Sachsen and Brandenburg turnout fell in each case by over ten per cent, and in these three Länder lay under the 60 per cent level.

Thus the trend, visible since the middle of the 1980s, towards increasing abstention in elections at all levels continued in *Superwahljahr*. This strong increase in non-voting – one of the most prominent political phenomena of recent years – was first noticeable in the Bundestag election of 1987. In the years following, turnout fell in many and various elections in Germany to record low levels not experienced for decades. In the new Länder also, once the euphoria of reunification and the 'novelty effect' had disappeared, enthusiasm about voting swiftly and markedly diminished.

In aggregate, all this indicated a reversal of a development which had lasted for over a century in Germany. After the introduction of universal male suffrage (women were enfranchised in 1919) turnout had generally increased relatively continuously; for example, turnout in the Reichstag election of 1871 was 51 per cent, increasing over the years to the 91.1 per cent turnout in the 1972 Bundestag election. It then remained around this high level for more than a decade, until in the Bundestag elections of 1987 and 1990 a reverse trend became apparent, a trend which in 1994 was recently confirmed.

The Quality of a Democracy is not Measured by Electoral Turnout

Not only the notion, referred to at the beginning of this article, that the trend of abstentionism was halted in 1994 is thus premature. The conclusion derived from it: that the German political system is consequently strengthened, cannot be supported by this argument. For the level of electoral turnout in itself can hardly be taken as evidence regarding the quality of a democratic system and the democratic maturity of its citizens. It is just those 'classical' democracies such as the USA and Switzerland which one would scarcely categorise as 'worse' democratic systems simply on account of their markedly lower rates of electoral participation. Just as obviously, the electors in the Saarland are not therefore 'better' democrats simply because in that Land electoral turnout traditionally is considerably higher than it is, for instance, in Baden-Württemberg.

How high a 'proper' level of electoral turnout should be cannot be determined normatively. The judgement depends – as cannot be too often emphasised in relation to factual discussion of non-voting – on the democratic-theory perspective which is employed. According to the input-oriented theory of democracy, the views and wishes of all citizens should contribute to the political process, and the elected legislature should be as thoroughly representative as possible. The act of voting becomes valuable in itself, and maximum electoral participation is sought. Abstention would thus be evaluated altogether negatively. In contrast, the output-oriented theory of democracy regards elections as a means to an end: power is transferred thereby, and the effectiveness of the system is in this way guaranteed. A high level of turnout is therefore not necessary. An optimum level of electoral participation should be expected. Abstention, according to this theory, can be useful, especially if practised by those who do not correspond to the ideal image of a 'politically mature, responsible citizen'.

It is no accident that the German proportional-representation electoral system, much more than the British majoritarian electoral system, emphasises the input perspective and stresses 'equitable' representation rather than 'governability'; the German democratic spirit appears indeed to be more idealistic than the rather pragmatic spirit of British democrats. Therefore the opinion that a high level of turnout demonstrates how stable a political system is and how democratically minded are its people is nowhere as widespread as it is in Germany.

It is above all vital to understand how, in going back over a nearly two-year period, such an agitated concern about *Politikverdrossenheit* could exist. After all, in view of what has already been stated, it can surprise nobody that the decline in general enthusiasm about elections is perceived by the general public and also by many political figures as a sign of crisis. The resulting zealous search for the causes of this purported crisis promotes the so-called *Politikverdrossenheit* of the Germans probably more than much that is in the end discovered by that search.

There is No Such Thing as the 'Party of Non-Voters'

The idea of a widespread *Politikverdrossenheit* is fostered by the misleading concept of the 'party of non-voters'. Convenient though this term is (and it is particularly favoured by the mass media), it is nonetheless false, because it conjures up a homogeneity which, first, does not exist, and which, second, is interpreted in a particular way. By use of the term: 'party of non-voters' a distinction is drawn *vis-à-vis* the 'other' parties; the 'non-voters' must then be dissatisfied with these 'other' parties, or else they would turn out to vote.

In actuality, the non-voters even in *Superwahljahr* 1994 are not a 'party', but rather a grouping which is differently constituted from one election to the next. The only thing which links non-voters is the fact that they do not turn out to vote! There are non-voters who cannot really be counted as such: the apathetic; the sick; those absent on journies; the lonely; and many others. On this account, not every act of non-voting can be regarded as an act of protest and thus be considered to contribute to the conclusions drawn from abstentionism.

Even in the period of greater electoral enthusiasm in Germany a varied set of causes led to abstention in elections: for example errors on the electoral register. The officially declared statistics of electoral turnout based on the number of those qualified to vote and on the number of votes actually recorded were in principle always below the actual level of turnout. For instance, between the compilation of the electoral register and election day several of those qualified to vote would have died or changed residence, yet would have been recorded as non-voters. Added to these 'false non-voters' are both the 'involuntary non-voters': those who fall ill at the time of the election or who are on journies away from home, and who have no opportunity (except by taking utterly excessive measures) to cast their vote, and the postal voters whose vote is not delivered in time or is not accompanied by the necessary polling card. The sum of all these non-voters can be estimated as totalling between about four and five per cent of the registered electorate, so that in the Federal Republic a maximum participation rate of only about 95 per cent is attainable.

This all has not the slightest connection with *Politikverdrossenheit*: that is, with the generalised feeling of dissatisfaction of whatever nature with politicians and parties. With appropriate adjustments, this is valid also for the central causes of recent increases in abstention rates, including those in 1994.

The most significant causes of reduced political participation as presented in the following comments on the links between *Politikverdrossenheit* and abstention are derived largely from a broad-based empirical investigation conducted in Stuttgart after the 1990 Bundestag election.

To obtain answers concerning the various motivations of non-voters and voters, a representative sample of over 20,000 selected citizens were questioned in a postal survey. About two-thirds of these participated in the investigation. In the end, responses of 5,336 voters and 2,116 non-voters were analysed.

No Participation Without Integration

The idealistic image is that of the 'enlightened citizen' deciding after mature reflection and uninfluenced consideration for or against voting, and for which party or candidate. The reality can be very different. Electoral behaviour is very often group behaviour, recognisable as such for example by the fact that many voters do not visit the polling station on their own. Indeed, the 'decision' for or against casting one's vote is in many cases in itself no decision at all – electoral participation or abstention can be the result of relatively accidental choices. In the collective activity of 'going to vote' and in some circumstances even when the vote itself is an individual action, a more strongly motivated voter can involve other voters in that activity. To an extent because of this, married voters (or those living in relationships similar to the married state) always turn out to vote in markedly higher numbers than 'singles' living alone, those who are divorced, or widowed persons. On these grounds, the tendency to turn out to vote increases with the number of persons living in the household. The difference is especially pronounced between single-person and two-person households.

According to results from the survey, there seems to be little relationship between family status and size of household on the one hand, and interest in, or evaluation of, politics on the other. It indicates the positive influence of 'feelings of security' on the readiness to go to vote, via a straightforward 'accompaniment effect' as well as the not inconsiderable effect of 'social pressure': registered voters with existing, but not strong, motivations to participate in elections become literally 'fellow-travellers' if persons close to them go to vote. The more people who constitute one's immediate circle and the closer are the associative ties, the greater is the chance that, in the event of one's own stimulus to go to vote being insufficient, a decisive external impulse will succeed in producing voting participation.

With reference to turnout, social ties in general play an important role. The readiness of a registered voter actually to go to vote is the greater the more contact to other persons which the voter possesses, and the greater the part he or she plays in society's activities. It is not therefore very astonishing to find that the tendency to vote in elections is greater in a community or town, the fewer the inhabitants which it possesses. As a rule, increasing size of a community leads to increased anonymity and a reduction in the number of interpersonal contacts. For the same reason, the willingness to vote increases also with the length of residence for inhabitants of a community: the longer someone has lived in a community or town, the more he or she can feel 'rooted' and socially integrated there.

Isolation encourages electoral abstention, and not only in the case of older people. An especially restricted level of participation in elections can be observed in the case of obviously underprivileged groups such as the Indian or black sections of society in the USA and socially marginal groups. An extreme example in Germany is the homeless.

The dynamic of individualisation in society is not confined to the family. In similar fashion, links to the churches, trade unions, voluntary associations and other organisations are diminishing, and with them the levels of electoral turnout. The positive relationship between willingness to vote and engagement in associations and other organisations is confirmed by the replies of the Stuttgart respondents. What is surprising to note is not so much the extent to which willingness to vote on the part of those who are not members of associations differs from the willingness of members of associations, as rather how such willingness to vote increases further with increases in the number of associations to which a respondent belongs.

It seems baffling that activities in associations can for their members, in contrast to other family members or other members of the household, act as 'consciousness-raising', and that incentives to participate in elections therefore are not confined to external stimuli. With membership in one or more associations, according to survey responses, the interest in politics and the degree of internalisation of the norm of electoral participation (voluntary associations being 'motors of mobilisation') increased almost linearly. In addition, associations can show themselves to be 'image improvers'; members of associations were much less ready to express ideas associated with *Politikverdrossenheit* than were non-members.

The result of all this is that absent or scarcely existent social integration is one of the main factors in the explanation of electoral abstention. The general decline in participation at elections in the Federal Republic is therefore caused to a considerable degree by the decrease in social ties and so to an extent is the logical and normal consequence of social developments. In the longer term, the increase in abstention for these causes will surely continue, since an end to, let alone a reversal of, the processes which lead to more and more disintegration is not in sight. Individualism advances onwards, and institutions such as the churches, associations and the family, whose activities have positive consequences for the inclination of the individual to participate in elections, continue to lose their influence. The act of voting is no longer a civic duty. The findings discussed above are not completely novel. Their significance, though, acquires current emphasis in view of the decrease in social ties. It is necessary to stress this because it is important for the conclusions which can be drawn from the increase in electoral abstention even in 1994: that not every non-voter is affected by *Politikverdrossenheit*.

So to assess the increase in numbers of non-voters as in the first instance the result of a normalisation process, especially in terms of international comparison, is also to say that participation in elections is less and less regarded as a civic duty. The strong social norm of having to go to vote was for decades a characteristic of the political culture of the Federal Republic, and decisively contributed to the extremely high levels (in international comparison) of electoral turnout.

Today, in part as a consequence of value-change, the *right* to vote is far less frequently regarded as an *obligation* to vote. This is the more obvious, the younger the member of the electorate is. The outcome is that various and often mundane causes, which in previous times would not have prevented anyone from going to vote, now lead to electoral abstention.

The Selective Non-Voter

As has been demonstrated, there are several aspects which point to a more relaxed evaluation, if not a total downplaying, of the increase in non-voting. Of course, this does not mean that it can be regarded as a matter of no consequence whatsoever. Certainly growing electoral abstention constitutes a symptom of crisis, because there now exists a new type of non-voter, which until the middle of the 1980s in Germany was hardly visible.

Until that time, non-voting was regarded as a function of the level of interest in politics: high levels of interest led to voting, lower levels to abstention. This tendency was valid even when – especially in the early years of the Federal Republic – there were more voters than there were citizens with an interest in politics. Abstention, when it existed, was not really perceived as a conscious act of political behaviour.

As before, one can state that the more a citizen is interested in politics and the more he informs himself about politics, the greater is the probability that he will participate in elections. However, the reverse is of limited predictive value: a pronounced interest in politics no longer involves the act of voting as an automatic consequence.

Certainly not the non-voter as such, but rather a new type of non-voter is distinguished by a strong interest in politics. Electoral abstention as the result of a conscious political decision of the politically interested and well-informed citizen is, in addition to the decline of social integration, the second central cause of a general reduction in electoral participation. More and more non-voters are 'voters' in this sense of selecting abstention as a deliberate choice. An indication of this can also be found in the fact that, despite the steady increase in levels of education and despite the oft-proven general increase in interest in politics in Germany, there has been this decline in electoral participation as already described.

When in other studies the numbers of these politically interested, consciously selective non-voters appear to be negligible, or their existence even denied altogether, this is principally because it is just these non-voters who tend in surveys to adapt themselves to the social norm of 'the obligation to vote', and therefore give false responses. The Stuttgart survey in 1991 was the first in Germany to succeed in using the electoral register to check on answers given by respondents. By this means it was established that more than a quarter of known non-voters who took part in the survey gave false answers. More important still, it was those with well above average interest in politics, conscious 'protest non- voters', who concealed their abstentionism because they especially approved of the norm of electoral participation and who therefore had an uneasy conscience.

What is this protest directed against? Reasons given by 'voting' non-voters for their subjective discontent referred usually to: political scandals and affairs ('they're all corrupt'); politicians being distant from the people ('those up there do what they want'); unresolved problems and lack of political alternatives ('the parties are all the same'); in brief, everything that one readily associates with the done-to-death term, *Politikverdrossenheit*. Abstention from voting has become a new outlet for the assuredly not-new phenomenon of *Politikverdrossenheit*. What is quite astonishing as well is the fact that this diffuse discontent reveals itself more as a social status-related than an age-specific problem. The image of corrupt and low-quality politicians, and belief in one's own powerlessness, are above all widespread among the 'ordinary folk', which is certainly one of the reasons why among blue-collar workers, for example, the tendency to abstain from voting, as well as what is often the next step: protest voting, have increased.

Electoral abstention as a form of political 'vote' nevertheless lost some of its significance in 1994 in comparison to previous years, because many citizens have tended to use those elections which they regard as less important and which are separated by some distance in time from the Bundestag election, to abstain deliberately from voting or to use the ballot paper for experimentation. Equally, it appears that many citizens who in 1990–93 gave expression at every opportunity to their *Politikverdrossenheit* came instead to question the reasons for their subjective dissatisfaction. It is after all hardly possible to hold politicians and parties responsible for everything of which they stand accused! To explain the rise in *Politikverdrossenheit* and the resulting abstentionism, one must look, in part at least, to an altered perspective on political phenomena which the mass media and the public have acquired, and to processes of change in foreign and domestic politics which have brought with them loss of orientation, a decline in public spiritedness, and perhaps exaggerated expectations of what politics can achieve.

That there exists no logical connection between objective grievances and the *Politikverdrossenheit* and abstentionism which result from those grievances reveals one thing at least: many non-voters say that they abstain from voting because there are too many polarising conflicts. Others, on the other hand, complain that the parties are all the same, and that well-defined party identities and clear differences between the parties are lacking.

The increase in non-voting is, also in *Superwahljahr* 1994, certainly in part a symptom of crisis, but mainly also a manifestation of a process of normalisation. Germany must become accustomed to lower levels of electoral participation, which will anyway continue to decline because of the erosion of social ties. But one should not always glorify this as *Politikverdrossenheit* or search for that phenomenon in accordance with the motto: 'where there are non-voters, there also must exist *Politikverdrossenheit*.' For Germany's parties, non-voters, and the mobilisation of those non-voters in electoral campaigns, will remain as a central challenge.

NOTES

1. The term *Politikverdrossenheit* is hard to translate successfully. It indicates an alienation from politics, politicians and parties, and a frustration with the political process.

Media Communication and Personality Marketing: The 1994 German National Election Campaign[1]

BERNHARD BOLL

This article concentrates on the parties' organisational and strategic techniques for the German national election campaign 1994. By analysing the parties' approaches for the set-up of the campaign, it is argued that modern media usage and personalised strategies will increasingly prevail in modern election campaigns. Moreover, the article confirms the persistence of a still-existing electoral gap in terms of communicational habits between east and west Germans. While some parties attempted an identical campaign throughout the country, they were forced to complete their activities by adopting techniques exclusively used in the east.

The National Context: The Super-Election-Year 1994

Chronologically, the second all-German elections of 16 October 1994 were no more than the final cut in an almost endless scenery of elections. In total, the so-called 'super-election-year 1994' comprised 19 elections at all governmental levels in Germany, and were supposed to change the political landscape significantly. In early March, Gerhard Schröder's electoral triumph in Lower Saxony, which allowed him to govern without Bündnis 90/Die Grünen, the SPD's former coalition partner, seemed to be the starting point of what was thought to be the decline of the Kohl era. Before and during the first quarter of the year, survey reports showed the Kohl administration and the chancellor himself hopelessly rejected by the electorate. Ever since the beginning of 1993, polls reported a huge advantage for Social Democratic candidate Rudolf Scharping, who was significantly more favoured in comparison to Helmut Kohl, as respondents were asked about their preferred candidate for the chancellorship. Hence, for the Social Democrats, the upcoming elections seemed to be logical steps on their way to power on the national level.

In May, the attention of the German population was additionally attracted by the election of the new President of the Federal Republic of

Germany, Roman Herzog, through the Bundesversammlung in Berlin. In principle, the formally independent Bundesversammlung could have also elected the immensely popular Social Democratic candidate, Johannes Rau. The SPD's belief in this chance was obviously even stronger than its clear-headed calculation of predominating coalitional ties; thus, after the election of Herzog, an irritated German public observed a furious Scharping who rather naively blamed the FDP for having voted in accordance with its Bonn coalitional partner instead of voting for Rau. The first nationwide electoral event, the European elections on 12 June, also did not bring about an electoral change in favour of the Social Democrats. Rather surprisingly, polls showed chancellor Kohl's CDU taking the lead. At that time, the economic boom that had started during autumn 1993 had boosted Kohl's reputation, increasingly so the more the recession was thought to have ended.

The Land elections in Sachsen-Anhalt one month later, on 26 June, were therefore considered not only as the last test of voters' preferences before the national parliamentary summer break. Similar to the European elections, the results of these Land elections were hoped by the SPD to signal nationwide a definite electoral change in favour of the Social Democrats. The conditions for such an enterprise seemed fairly good: Sachsen-Anhalt had experienced two resignations of Christian Democratic prime ministers due to financial or political scandals. Its coalition partner, the FDP, was close to intra-party disruption and therefore not a very attractive option even for the liberal electorate. Electoral results, however, led to a tied situation. The CDU (34.4 per cent) was no longer able to continue its coalition government with the FDP, who had failed to re-enter the Landtag with a mere 3.6 per cent. On the other hand, the heir to the former socialist state party, the PDS, finished with 19.9 per cent. Also, a sobering share of 34 per cent for the SPD and a no less disappointing 5.1 per cent for Bündnis 90/Die Grünen did not enable the SPD to take over government with the Greens alone. Instead, a coalition was formed by the Social Democrats and Bündnis 90/Die Grünen, tolerated by the PDS. This tacit tolerance of a left-wing minority coalition by the PDS, the so-called 'Magdeburg Model', was to have a major impact on the national campaign. The Magdeburg Model was welcomed by the Conservatives as a rather unexpected electoral asset which allowed them to polarise electoral opinions between them and the looming 'people's front' of SPD, Bündnis 90/Die Grünen and the PDS.

From that point, the CDU instrumentalised the SPD's alleged political *faux pas* for its own campaign, playing a risky game in terms of the different political perceptions in the new and the old Länder. The CDU blamed the SPD for the silent agreement with that 'party *non grata*' on the Land level, for having broken the 'democratic consensus' of the established parties to isolate the PDS. For the rest of the time until the Bundestag elections, the CDU's 'red-socks campaign' endlessly emphasised the fact that the model would also serve as a matrix for the national level and irresponsibly bring back the socialist PDS to governmental power.

These allegations were differently perceived in both parts of the new Germany. In the east, even amongst the officials of the CDU, the hypocritical tone of the campaign was heavily criticised. After all, the campaign also touched upon the past of many east German CDU-members who themselves were not inclined to deny their former political sympathies. According to a poll of August 1994, 71 per cent of east Germans still believed that socialism was a good idea simply badly performed, while 40 per cent of east Germans liked the idea that the PDS should again be represented in the 13th Bundestag.[2]

In the western part of the country, the success of the PDS provoked uncertainty and fear of a German socalist renaissance within the bourgeois strata. Additionally, the comeback of the socialist PDS not only in Sachsen-Anhalt, but also in the Land elections of 11 September in Sachsen and Brandenburg, met irritation amongst wide sections of the west German population. On one side, many criticised the rather crude terminology: for example, the CSU in Bayern even had Karl Marx on billboards greeting his readers with 'I am back in Sachsen-Anhalt!', while the CDU in Mecklenburg-Vorpommern presented the SED's old symbol, the socialist handshake between KPD and SPD and warned 'Never ever again!'. Yet on the other hand, after three successful results for the PDS in the new Länder, the campaign seemed to express a diffuse impression in the west of an intransigent socialist nostalgia and a perpetuating political naivety of the '*Ossis*'.

Coalition Formulae

As regards the party system and the chances of a governmental change, the campaign served quite other functions. Since the notion of a tied race between government and opposition did not completely fade away even with the perception of economic growth and increasing individual optimism, the red-socks campaign could also be seen as a cynical but efficient additional means to weaken the SPD.

After all, it had become apparent that Kohl's chances for survival depended particularly on the fate of the smaller parties and the resulting coalition options in the new Bundestag. In the eastern part of Germany, the campaign would not polarise between SPD and CDU. It would rather provoke the electoral differentiation between SPD and CDU as western parties on one side, and a genuine east German party like the PDS with an exclusive articulation of eastern interests on the other. Arguably, a stabilised PDS was in the interest of the CDU for the following two reasons. At best, the campaign would weaken the SPD in the west (as a result of anti-communist reflexes) and also in the east, because many voters would directly vote for the PDS – not least as an expression of their east German identity. With the PDS in parliament, it was more likely that the old coalition would be able to continue than be changed by a SPD–Bündnis 90/Die Grünen coalition. The second-best outcome for the CDU would be a loss of its strategic majority in the Bundestag, that is, the impossibility of forming a government without the CDU/CSU parliamentary party. However, the successful marginalisation of the PDS through the red-socks campaign would not have allowed anything other than a grand coalition.

The red-socks campaign troubled the SPD significantly. Party representatives needed to defensively and continually repeat that the SPD would not co-operate in Bonn with the PDS on the basis of the Magdeburg model. Thus, the party was more involved in defending itself against these allegations than in a politically aggressive discourse with the governing coalition parties. Furthermore, in terms of coalition arithmetic, a coalition between a moderately strengthened SPD and Bündnis 90/Die Grünen would not have the majority needed to form a government in Bonn. Moreover, the FDP had clearly committed itself against a so-called 'Ampel-Koalition', consisting of the SPD, Bündnis 90/Die Grünen and the FDP. Thus, the Magdeburg model, thought of as a demonstration of offensive will, turned out to straitjacket the SPD. Captured in a completely defensive and unfavourable strategic position, the primary goal of the Social Democrats, to oust Kohl from office, seemed next to impossible if coalitional options were included in the calculus. From this perspective, the campaign was a clear instrumentalisation of the east in order to guarantee the success of the CDU/CSU in the west.

It was clear that the PDS, in turn, would profit in the east from the CDU's provocative campaign. Nevertheless, even with an electoral share of about 20 per cent in all Land elections in eastern Germany, it was by no means clear whether the PDS would be represented in the next Bundestag by jumping over the five per cent hurdle nationwide. The PDS's calculus was therefore based on another regulation of the German Election Law. The latter stipulates that three directly won mandates circumvented the five per cent hurdle by qualifying parties (and in this case the PDS) to participate in the proportional distribution of further Bundestag seats via the party's Land lists. Hence, from the very beginning of the electoral campaign, the PDS especially nurtured its strongholds in the eastern Berlin outskirts, where three direct mandates seemed most likely to be won.

By the end of what was called by some observers,[3] 'an election

TABLE 1

BUNDESTAG ELECTION RESULTS 1990 AND 1994

Bundestag	Seats 1994	Seats 1990	Second Votes 1994 (%)	Second Votes 1990 (%)
CDU/CSU	294	319	41,4	43,8
SPD	252	239	36,4	33,5
FDP	47	79	6,9	11,0
B'90/Die Grünen	49	8	7,3	5,1
PDS	30	17	4,4	2,4
Others	–	–	3,6	4,2

Source: Forschungsgruppe Wahlen (FGW), 1994, p.6–8.

campaign of cultivated boredom', on election day nobody was really surprised to see the CDU/CSU losing votes but able to continue the coalition with a massively weakened FDP that triumphantly celebrated itself and its parliamentary survival. The election results (see Table 1) showed that the coalition majority had melted down to ten seats more than those of the SPD, Bündnis 90/Die Grünen, and the PDS combined. Only the addition of 12 *Überhangmandate* (additional seats) gained by the CDU/CSU (compared to only four won by the SPD) gave the coalition a more comfortable majority. Without these surplus mandates, the Kohl coalition would only have had a majority of two Bundestag seats after the elections.

Campaign Organisation and Control

The first steps towards what might be called campaign activity for the 1994 Bundestag elections were taken at different times by every party. As early as 1992, the FDP and the PDS thought about national election campaigning, while the SPD did so from October of the same year onwards. By contrast, neither the central campaign committee of Bündnis 90/Die Grünen, nor the CDU headquarter personnel formally met for the first time before autumn 1993.

CDU

The CDU's so-called '*kleine Lage*' campaign team consisted of about ten persons who worked out general concepts and slogans of the campaign.

Members of this circle were the business manager of the party and the heads of the departments of finance and administration, organisation, and politics. Additionally, the office managers of the party chairman, Helmut Kohl, that of the general secretary, Peter Hintze, and two representatives of the party programme commission participated in a bigger group which was in charge of the conceptualisation and monitoring of the campaign. Also, the business manager of the party directed the CDU's public relations department throughout the campaign, including the contacts to pollsters that accompanied the party's entire campaign from the beginning. After budgetary and logistic questions were settled on a preliminary basis, marketing companies were invited to make presentations. Finally, three differently specialised marketing companies were given contracts, with one company taking the conceptional lead of the other two. Towards the end of this process, in early 1994, the complete campaign concept was then taken for decision to the national Executive committee chaired by Helmut Kohl, which finally decided upon the campaign strategy. Thus, the threefold division of labour that had already been observed in the 1990 campaign was also undertaken in 1994.[4]

Survey results showed a rather disadvantageous climate for the party at the beginning of 1994. Therefore, it was decided to attack the political adversary aggressively during the entire campaign. Also, even though Kohl's popularity was at a low point, an intensive personalised campaign, featuring the personal quality and the political experience of chancellor Helmut Kohl, was agreed upon as early as October 1993 for the Bundestag elections.[5] Because public opinion altered in favour of Kohl about the time of the European elections in June (see Figure 1), the party already began to promote Kohl intensively though he did not run for any European office. Even though the party's strategy for the European elections was not especially concentrated on Kohl, an additional personal emphasis of the campaign emerged during the summer and was fully in place during the 'hot phase' of the campaign from mid-September 1994. Without any slogan, Kohl appeared omnipresently and nationwide on large billboards and placards, showing merely (a delicately magnified) smiling chancellor Kohl in the midst of enthusiastic masses.

During the entire election year, Kohl's central campaign position was emphasised by 114 events at which he spoke (allegedly mostly to organised and 'drafted' party members) particularly in east Germany. In total, the speech-delivering campaign of Kohl alone cost DM 6 million out of a DM 70 million total budget for the Bundestag elections. In Bavaria, the conservative CSU campaigned independently on the basis of a common election platform, which was agreed upon with the CDU in August 1994. With a DM 14 million budget, the CSU performed a combined, rather

FIGURE 1

ELECTORAL PREFERENCE FOR CHANCELLERY: KOHL VERSUS SCHARPING NOVEMBER 1993 THROUGH OCTOBER 1994

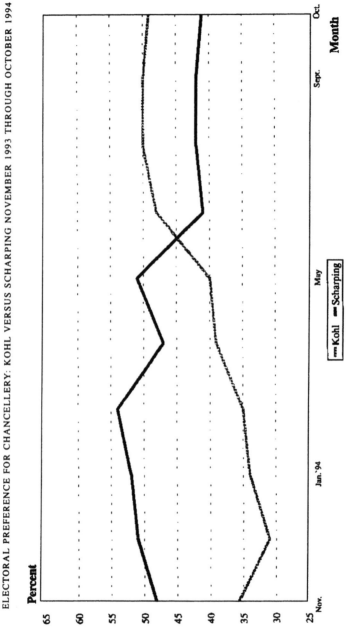

Kohl ——Scharping

Source: Politbarometer, Forschungsgruppe Wahlen Mannheim, in: *Süddeutsche Zeitung*, 1993, 1994, various issues.

identical Land and national election campaign with only marginal changes, due to the tight schedule of the Land election on 25 September and the Bundestag election 16 October 1994.

Intra-party mobilisation and control of the CDU was achieved through the conference of Land party organisation managers. During the entire campaign, the conference met five times to brief campaigners about the party's strategy. Headed by the national party business manager, a description of the strategy was followed by a discussion and instruction about the most efficient means to perform the campaign successfully. Additionally, 13 regional conferences were organised to disseminate the strategy of the party's headquarters.[6] Participants not only included Land party managers, but also the chairmen and members of the Land party executives, regional party chairmen and the individual candidates.

To guarantee a nationwide uniform appearance of the central party's campaign, every regional party unit was supplied free of charge with 10,000 leaflets with the portrait of Kohl, 3,500 posters featuring the national party, and, additionally, 3,000 copies of Kohl-posters, 'people's front', and general testimony posters. Above all, lower level party units could order small articles and give-aways at their own charge via the branch offices of a supply company to complete their campaign activities. Intra-party network communication is not yet entirely set up at all levels of the CDU. 'Comsys', an internal mail-box and data system, is being established, but was not in use generally. However, at least all Länder and a significant part of all regional party organisations are plugged into the network. Particularly the new party organisations in east Germany were to be attached to this system.

In general, mass media were intensively used by the CDU. Three different radio spots were produced to be broadcast by public stations. Broadcast 76 times on television, one out of two 2.5-minute spots, titled 'our chancellor', showed Kohl with leading international politicians as a considerate agent of public needs; this spot was transmitted by the public TV stations. Additionally, a selection of 15 CDU spots (30 seconds) were aired 620 times via private radio stations focusing on special topics. Kohl himself was especially featured by SAT 1, a private TV station.[7] Attention was paid to certain private TV stations being watched by a potential CDU electorate. Besides the number of spots and their appropriate messages, the correct timing before and after special shows was important to the party's media specialists. Spots were placed before or after those movies which were assumed to be watched by the clientele most in favour of the CDU, or as yet undecided but with a potential tendency towards the party. In contrast to the eight rather long (2.5 minutes) spots on the public TV stations, the 30-second spots broadcast by private channels proved to be a surprisingly flexible instrument. For example, during the European election campaign, such a spot was discussed and conceptualised during the morning hours in the Bonn headquarters and broadcast the same day at prime time around 7 p.m.[8]

In addition, the CDU attempted a quasi-interactive telephone event, subtitling a Bonn-based number ('0228-1994') in every spot to be called for further information and, though not guaranteed, for direct contact to leading CDU politicians.[9]

SPD

Basically, the pillars of the Social Democratic campaign strategy were worked out in a closed meeting that lasted several days. This meeting included the business manager of the SPD, Günther Verheugen, and his department heads (communication and elections, finance, politics); additionally, researchers and consultants were invited to debate the strategy during November 1992. Also, a marketing company that had already been selected in 1988 for the creation of the party's corporate image, participated in the meeting. In order to find the best fit for campaign activities, important 'communicational events' inside and outside politics were assembled in a 'campaign calendar'. This included, for example, major sports and cultural events, controversial legislative projects towards the end of the legislative period, and the last parliamentary debate before election day. Also, on the basis of empirical research results, the themes and issues to be articulated and the instruments to be used to present the party were selected during this closed meeting. The resulting preliminary campaign concept was presented for decison to the national executive committee chaired by Rudolf Scharping. Towards the end of 1993, a technical commission was established to co-ordinate logistic and organisational questions of the campaign.

Qualitatively, the SPD had ordered a survey with about 200 in-depth interviews. Members of target groups were interviewed to find out about the latest, most articulated problems and images of the party and its candidate. After all, the SPD had lost its candidate-to-be and former chairman Björn Engholm through his resignation in May 1993. Therefore, the party had only little more than a year in which to create and promote the personal image of its new chancellor-candidate, Rudolf Scharping. Thus, a differentiated test of Rudolf Scharping's popularity was performed, showing that increasing positive evaluations of the candidate emerged even amongst conservative respondents if more information about his personal background was made available.

The 1994 campaign of the SPD showed a strong development towards personalisation and media usage. Not only as a clear and direct answer to the highly personalised Kohl campaign of the CDU, as Verheugen later declared, a Scharping personality-spot was produced. Also, as an empirically tested means to promote Scharping, a 2.5-minute spot with a strong biographical note was presented by Scharping himself and broadcast by using the free time given to the SPD on both public TV stations. In addition to other newspaper and magazine advertisements, about 300 30-second spots were broadcast by private TV stations. In general, the SPD operated with a common nationwide concept of the campaign. However, in the eastern part of the country other issues were emphasised and other instruments used. Due to the ongoing membership (and hence: activist) weakness of the party, print media were used nearly on a daily basis, amplified by almost equally frequent radio spots.

Intra-party communication and control were performed in six different ways. A public mailbox system connected individuals directly to the SPD Bundestag parliamentary party's information system. Also, via an integrated fax system, all SPD party organisations down to the district level were supplied with information and data from the SPD headquarters. Thirdly, additional information was presented with the traditional newspaper for members, *Vorwärts*, and, for campaigners and party officials only, via a magazine called *intern*. A fourth communication means was a telephone hotline which was operated almost on a 24-hour basis in order to guarantee quick and permanent assistance for campaigners. Moreover, a public mailbox system that served as an information pool was used for quick and efficient data exchange with the party's headquarters. Finally, a data base on diskette for all party organisations was offered. It included, besides pre-formatted leaflets, a selection of articles suitable to be printed in party constituency newspapers and suchlike.

All this was framed into a regular, monthly rhythm of meetings of national campaigners with those from Land and district levels to discuss, improve and feed back the on-going campaign activities. The SPD's DM 70 million Bundestag campaign was officially started with the campaign's opening event in Bonn on 9 August 1994. The headquarters financially supported every Bundestag election constituency with about DM 20–30,000. In addition, free posters also paid for by party headquarters guaranteed equal visibility of the party throughout Germany.

FDP

The FDP had begun to conceptualise its campaign strategy as early as 1992. Similar in size and structure to thoses of the other parties, the Liberals' campaign committee originally planned a concept that concentrated on only a few top issues. With topics related to economic policy and another classical liberal policy field, legal issues, the FDP's corporate image which was intended to emerge from those topics would be used in all electoral campaigns of 1994. Thus, in contrast to other parties, the national executive of the FDP had decided to conceptualise one general approach, with only marginal deviations of content during all the respective nationwide, Land or local elections. To get the message across the country, a marketing concept was worked out towards the end of 1993 by an agency that traditionally promotes the party. During the first quarter of the following year, the dramatic slogan for the Bundestag election campaign ('Diesmal geht's um alles') was also decided upon and integrated in the campaign. Similar to the 1990 campaign of the party, much of the party's campaign activity concentrated on conventional means like newspaper advertisements, billboards and placards and so on.

Conceptually, the seemingly monolithic campaign strategy of the party was born out of a combination of two aspects. First, because of an almost invisible, or at best confusing, image of the party: amongst wide parts of the German electorate, the FDP was increasingly perceived as a coalitional party without any specific political, liberal quality. Secondly, for budgetary reasons, only a financially limited campaign budget of the national party was available. For both the European and the national campaign, the FDP headquarters spent DM 20 million in total, with a DM 14 million share for the national campaign. For the national campaign, every national election constituency was supplied with campaign material cheques, worth DM 1,500 each, enabling them to buy campaign items on the national party's account at their own convenience. Moreover, target groups were wooed: 200,000 direct mailings were sent to members of the professions (lawyers, doctors, architects and so on) and, for the first time for very many years, cinema advertising spots were screened to promote liberal ideas especially among the younger voters.

Intra-party organisation and control was less effective compared to the SPD and the CDU, since liberal Land party organisations cultivate a strongly independent and individual existence. Land party managers' conferences took place weekly before and during the 'hot phase' of the campaign. Nevertheless, though these meetings were intended to criticise and improve detected shortcomings of the campaign, the extent to which recommended remedies were integrated into the campaign remained subject to the decision of the individual Land party managers. Thus, the FDP's national party merely offered the assistance of the contracted marketing agency and the help of one former party officer who acted as a strategy consultant for the individual Land party organisation. Also, the party organised a nationwide campaign speech schedule of a dozen nationally ranked liberal politicians. For the benefit of a more or less identical campaign activity, all but the biggest liberal Land parties accepted the offer, if partially and reluctantly. Hence, basically, what was planned as a strategy of an emerging uniform image turned out to be a mix of Land and national parties' concepts. This questionable mixture particularly occurred in the new Land parties of the east (where the party was completely eliminated from all Land parliaments).

The question of the party's parliamentary future became more dramatic towards the last weeks of the national election campaign. After enormous losses in all Land elections up to that time, some liberal managers pulled the campaign emergency brakes by turning to old but well-known campaign techniques. Since the Land party organisation of Nordrhein-Westfalen, the biggest organisation, was very dissatisfied with the campaign strategy and the moderate campaigning of chairman Klaus Kinkel, it additionally featured a personalised campaign with elder party leaders like Hans-Dietrich Genscher, Otto Graf Lambsdorff, and of course, the *enfant terrible* and, during this time, chairman of the Land-FDP, Jürgen Möllemann.[10]

Due to financial limitations, the FDP neither employed pollsters for permanent empirical monitoring, nor was able to use electronic media on a larger scale. The party produced one spot to be used for the party's free broadcasting time in the public TV stations, and bought about two dozen 20-second spots aired on the comparatively cheap private news channel 'n-tv'. The FDP was the first party to operate an on-line computer network for data and information exchange in the west. Meanwhile, all Land party levels in the east and, in addition to that, even some local organisations in the West, are linked to this system. However, as party managers report, communications nevetherless took place mainly through 'traditional' means, for example, fax machines or telephone.

Bündnis 90/Die Grünen

At least between some of the Land party organisations of Bündnis 90/Die Grünen, a computer-based mailbox system is already in operation. Yet on a national scale, intra-party communication via an on-line network is still regarded with suspicion as another step towards intra-party centralisation. Instead, conventional telephone and fax lines were used to communicate in a campaign, whose primary goal was the return of the party to the Bundestag. The national election campaign committee that was set up in autumn 1993 had mainly operative and organisational responsibilities, whereas the members of the party's national executive were in charge of the political accentuation of the campaign. The national election campaign committee, whose members were appointed by the national executive, consisted of party functionaries of the national level, and representatives of eastern and western Land party organisations. During the campaign, however, only a reduced number of this circle worked permanently as 'operative staff members' in the headquarters of the party.

Bündnis 90/Die Grünen campaigned on the basis of a strictly decentralised structure. There was a clear-cut co-ordinatory and organisational division of labour between national and Land party levels. The national party was mainly in charge of a general campaign concept, technical organisation and advice, but had only limited opportunities to control directly the nationwide realisation of the campaign. Land organisations, on the other hand, completely organised, controlled (and paid for) their campaign activities. With the exception of east German Land party organisations, which were, in terms of organisation and membership, not strong enough to organise or to pay for their campaign, this division of labour was a general pattern of the Green campaign. To support eastern party organisations, campaign managers from other Land party organisations worked there from January through October 1994 on the Green campaign. Financially, the eastern Land parties were subsidised with about DM 50–60,000 per Land, which guaranteed minimum campaign activity at least.

The only direct communication between national and regional levels was a sort of technical manual for campaigners: in total about seven issues. By contrast to the first all-German campaign in 1990,[11] there was no centrally organised main campaign event like the 'purple caravan' or the 'climate express'. Instead, only some Land parties organised special-issue tours, for example, for women, for students or on general ecology issues of the region.

On the basis of empirical research which was asked for by the party for the first time, an analysis of electoral potentials was worked out and communicated to all party levels. Illustrated and conceptually enriched by a professional marketing agency, the analysis reflected the social structure of a potential Green electorate down to the constituency level and was thought to facilitate the identification of regions in which extra campaign activities would be promising. Beyond this, no other monitoring of media coverage or observations of pollsters was performed.

Nothing of the DM 4.9-million budget of the national party was spent on TV spots. Not even the free broadcasting time of the public stations was used for promotion. The four broadcasts on each of both public TV stations were reserved for the transmission of the winning anti-racism spots of a video contest, which the party had initiated amongst artists. The national party had paid for the production of posters ensuring a basic national representation of the party. Also, in poorly populated areas posters were installed and paid for by the national party in towns with less than 30,000 inhabitants. Though there was no differentiation in terms of campaign themes and instruments, at least in the east, some usage of modern media was deemed to be unavoidable. During the last week of the national campaign, initiated by the national party executive, 20 broadcast spots were aired in the new Länder to emphasise the significance of the second vote for Bündnis 90/Die Grünen. Also, in the east, the party additionally supported individual activists who erected posters based on any available topic with a good visibility in the new Länder.

In general, the party's main slogan ('Ein Land reformieren') appeared on every party poster. Three different subtitles to it were available, with usual Green issues, that is, ecology, peace, and equal rights of women, articulated. Very untypically, the party even showed tendencies towards a personalisation of the campaign, which up to then had been disgracefully banned as personal fetishism. This time, the party's most prominent figures, particularly Joschka Fischer, could be seen on placards both in the Land of his candidacy, Hesse, and in Nordrhein-Westfalen. The party did not succeed in organising a general campaign speech schedule. During the European elections, the party attempted a controlled schedule, but failed during the Bundestag campaign, because prominent speakers were usually already booked up. Though Land party campaign managers (particularly in the east) repeatedly asked for oratorical support, the prominent Greens obviously concentrated on their own Land campaigns, anxiously and diligently working on the party's goal in their (western) Länder.

PDS

By constrast, the PDS skilfully organised a two-fold campaign strategy for the old and new Länder from scratch. The party is almost exclusively organised in the east with still enormous membership figures and is extremely popular not only amongst the beneficiaries of the old system but also amongst disappointed east Germans, who feel themselves betrayed by German unification. Consequently, a split campaign emphasis and different campaign techniques are characteristic of the PDS's national campaign. Financially, in the new Länder, only DM 2.4 million were spent on the campaign budget, whereas DM 5.6 million were invested in the old Länder. Out of a total budget of DM 17 million for the entire super-election year, about DM 8 million were specifically devoted to the national election campaign.

Technically, the PDS performed a traditional, classic street-and-neighbourhood campaign in the east, and appeared almost exclusively on cinema screens, newspaper advertisments, student, sports, or gay magazines in the west. In the east, the campaign was thus fairly cheap, though the national party paid for the campaign completely. Land parties had to transfer a financial share to the national party and had to renounce all campaign revenues in favour of the national party. The national party sponsored the campaign totally and the personal membership network in the east was an almost costless resource. The old-fashioned mouth-to-mouth propaganda communicated by members was most welcomed and was most efficient, particularly amongst the elder party members and supporters. Even in Berlin, where the party had its best chances to win three direct seats, no extraordinary financial energy was needed (about DM 500,000 was spent) in order to mobilise members and supporters. Given the fact that in almost every East Berlin household PDS-members are present, a few central events and even moderate material and promotional proliferation of the party were obviously enough to keep PDS supporters and voters in good electoral spirits. The PDS also mounted a personalised campaign, concentrating important media or campaign events on the party's star, Gregor Gysi. An appealing figure among younger voters in both east and west Germany, only he among PDS politicians could draw the crowds, attracting a minimum of 1,000 listeners.

This two-fold campaign, technically and politically, was the result of what can be called a highly professionalised, minutely worked out campaign preparation. Similar to the FDP, the PDS started to work on a strategy in early spring 1992. The strategy being completed in November 1992, the simultaneous organisational set-up began by the establishment of a central election bureau in East Berlin. A discussion process with the national committee members and representatives of the Land parties about the draft strategy followed for the next five months. Involved were all sorts of party activists and scientists from Berlin universities of various disciplines: sociologists, economists and psychologists were among the consultants of the party as well as philosophers and philologists. Finally, in March 1993, a thoroughly discussed and improved draft was commissioned as the final conception of the party's 1994 national campaign. Seven marketing agencies, spread across the nation, contested for the campaign contract with the party, and an agency located in East Berlin was eventually awarded the contract.

Then regular empirical analysis of electoral attitudes was started, as an East Berlin-based institute was contracted to find out about perceptions of potential PDS voters on a quarterly basis. Additionally, a nationwide party image analysis was commissioned in August 1994. Consequently, during the entire period from March 1993 until the beginning of the hot phase of the campaign in August 1994, the party continously monitored its electoral prospects. In addition, east German Land election results yielded further information about the electoral strength of the PDS. Campaign control and some feed-back were achieved through different means. For the most part, advertisements in target group magazines asked for contact, which came to the attention of the party through numerous calls for further programmatic and political information. Also, via BTX, a public communication network, participants could not only simply read party information but were also able to ask questions which were answered more or less specifically.

Intra-party control was operated through regular meetings with the Land party campaign managers, and seminars were held to teach at least some parts of campaign knowledge. Generally, the latter was almost non-existent amongst lower (and older) party-level campaigners. In the western diaspora, a handful of campaigners could be found to work full time for the party in Bayern, Baden-Württemberg, Hamburg, and Niedersachsen, but particularly western students promoted the party on the basis of low-paid monthly contracts in the bigger cities. For the most part, in the old Länder, a media campaign was in operation. On TV, the party had a spot broadcast three times on public TV stations and by regional TV stations. A radio spot was produced and broadcast three times on average by various private and public radio stations. Eventually, regular, sometimes full-page, advertisements in the most important nationally distributed newspapers and magazines completed the media penetration of the PDS in the west.

Generally, young voters were the target group of the party. In cinemas, ironically styled tuned spots were shown, and on placards a mixture of erotic and political content promoted the correct electoral choice: 'while kissing – eyes closed, while voting – keep 'em open!' or: '63 per cent of all Germans would have an affair given a good opportunity – now here is one'. Older eastern party members were outraged by the strategy, but since they would stick to the party anyhow while enthusiastic comments fed back to the party via BTX, campaign strategists preferred to retain this style of campaigning.

The 1994 Campaign – Towards More Personalisation and Media Communication?

The most remarkable feature of the 1994 campaign was its truly unpolitical character. Though more than enough problems could have been the elements of a controversial public debate, a political discourse was virtually absent. The huge national deficit, the stability of the social security system or the still significant unemployment rate were neglected like cold thematical side orders alongside a main course of questions concerned with the political personnel.

It was only towards the beginning of the year that a potential change in government seemed likely. But the European elections results seemed to have completely deleted this important aspect. Instead, a remarkable decline of Scharping's popularity turned the attention of the public to the question whether Kohl would resign as chancellor midway through the following legislative period.

Yet, while not many seemed to be unhappy with Kohl's continuation, even fewer were thrilled by Scharping's appearance. Kohl's retrospective résumées of foreign policy successes and the promised (economic) blessings of German unification neither motivated nor convinced voters. Of course, Kohl avoided talking about the growing budget deficit, continued high unemployment rates in the East, or upcoming tax increases. But, paradoxically, while the public seemed to be tired of Kohl's promises and muddling-through style in the previous legislative period, the bigger part of it was not seriously debating a discontinuation of his style of government because the economic recession had been overcome and economically better times appeared to lie ahead.

The SPD, after all, largely failed to explain to the electorate why the propagated change in government should be so delightful to the country (*Freu' Dich auf den Wechsel, Deutschland!*) as its main slogan suggested. The Social Democrats were not able to launch any attractive or mobilising issues during the entire campaign. Moreover, even though the party's entire free public TV broadcasting time was spent on the promotion of the Social Democratic chancellor-candidate, Rudolf Scharping was neither able to convince the electorate as the younger personal alternative, nor could he escape from a publicly perceived image of a polite and diligent, yet uncharismatic and uninspiring politician.

Overall, the 1994 campaign was characterised by an intensive use of TV and new media by the parties which resulted in an increasingly personalised campaign. A personality campaign to an extent never seen before not only projected Kohl as the only individual choice of competence and quality. It also provoked other parties either to follow this path of a personalised campaign, or passively to lag behind it. Both strategies were performed for the parties' own good reasons. The CDU's decision to promote Kohl intensively was not a result of an ingenious coup by the party's strategists, but the considered step of a party that had previously been marginalised by its dominating chairman. By contrast, the SPD had to present a comparatively 'new' candidate who needed an equally frequent public appearance. Consequently, not only as a direct answer to the Kohl campaign, the Scharping campaign was needed as an additional impetus to create a strong personal alternative and promote an important part of the party's corporate image. The PDS also needed to participate in the personalisation game. Being the only representative of that party publicly known in the west, Gregor Gysi alone could guarantee the party's coverage by the media of the old Länder.

The FDP, for individual and financial reasons, could not actively participate and preferred to lag behind. Yet the Liberal antagonists, more or less unintentionally, found the media covering a special sort of personalised campaign. A generally unassuming Kinkel and a self-promoting Möllemann

FIGURE 2

MEDIA COVERAGE OF PARTY TOP CANDIDATES 1994 NATIONAL ELECTION CAMPAIGN

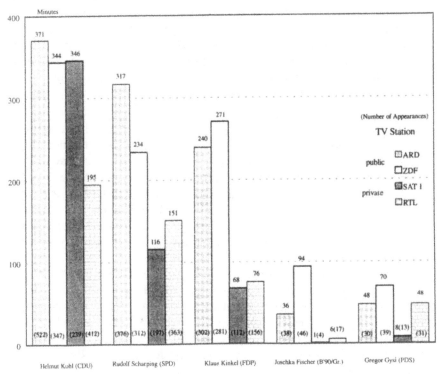

Source: Der Spiegel, No.40/1994, p.29

could permanently be observed debating, through interviews, the party's political appearance in general and strategy of its leaders. While Möllemann was preaching loyalty, he did not miss any opportunity subtly to undermine chairman Klaus Kinkel. Yet by doing so the FDP did not at all attract voters in order to strengthen liberalism, which, as the party argued, would be absolutely vital to German parliamentarism. What is more, these published intra-party intrigues rather posed the question of the future of a Liberal party in the German political system and it was probably the Liberals' continued emphasis on the party's function in German coalition politics that helped it over the five per cent hurdle.

Bündnis 90/Die Grünen, finally, was diligently working on its parliamentary comeback. But while there was still a neglect of the party's promotional appearance on the public TV stations, some steps towards personalisation and media appearance were nevertheless taken. With a more relaxed attitude of the rank-and-file towards the most prominent party figures, moderate attempts at efficient personal media appearance could be observed. Technically, it is interesting to look at the campaign strategies of the parties. All of them conceptualised a fully developed communication strategy. But, more than ever, media and personalisation were strongly emphasised. In retrospect, even in the 1990 campaign, an increasing tendency towards these two aspects could already be observed; and yet, during the 1990 campaign, traditional grassroots canvassing was still more important.[12] In the 1994 campaign, more diversified strategies were used. For example, the concentrated marketing of target groups by all parties, the use of direct mailings, telephone events, interactive media, mailbox and on-line systems, seemed to be particularly performed in the old Länder and demonstrated a strong tendency towards more modern campaign techniques. In the new Länder, however, old-fashioned face-to-face campaigning, as far as the organisational strength of the parties enabled them to, seemed to be more *á la mode* in a still modernising east German society. Moreover, while most parties had planned an identical campaign in both east and west, not only techniques but also issues still needed variation in the east.

The reasons for the observed changing accentuation are both financial and political. First, the costs for campaign rallies have significantly risen. The CDU, for example, spent as much as almost ten per cent of the national party's budget on Kohl's speech-delivering campaign. Secondly, the instrument seems increasingly to miss the goal: 'baptised supporters needn't be baptised any more' as one party campaigner described the rally situation. Apparently, only party members or followers attend the rally and thus demonstrate the parties' failed attempts to massively convince the unconvinced. This aspect might explain the exploding use of private TV and radio spots. Precisely timed and placed, they seem exactly to reach those who indifferently stayed at home. However, it does not mean that these are less receptive to campaign efforts than voters on the streets.

Yet, this strategy is not without ambivalence. Empirically, the 1990 media campaign shows that a more positive perception seems partially to emerge for politicians from their frequent apperance on a TV screen.[13] On the other hand, long-term empirical media content-analysis did not at all substantiate whether this campaign strategy really leads to a personalised voting.[14]

But no matter how, as long as parties believe that massive TV and radio campaign appearances are conducive to their means and ends, they will continue to spend intensively on it. Also, on-line systems and the like may constitute new forms of campaign communications. Consequently, since the screens of the new media require pictures and persons instead of problems the character of modern campaigns will probably increasingly change.

Arguably, even more diversified media communication and personality marketing will prevail in future campaigns.

NOTES

1. This article is based on interviews with the representatives of the parties: Friedrich Claudius Schlummbeger (CDU), Head of Organisation Department; Bernd Schoppe (SPD), Department Head Elections and Communications; Klaus Pfnorr (FDP), Head of Organisation Department; André Brie (PDS) member of the national executive and in charge of the party's campaign; Christoph Boppel (Bündnis 90/Die Grünen). For further data as well as critical comments, I am particularly indebted to Thomas Poguntke, University of Mannheim.
2. *Der Spiegel*, 15 Aug.1994, p.111.
3. Dieter Schröder, *Süddeutsche Zeitung*, 8/9 Oct.1994; Gunter Hoffmann, *Die Zeit*, 23 Sept. 1994, p.3; Theo Sommer, *Die Zeit*, 14 Oct. 1994, p.1.
4. Bernhard Boll and Thomas Poguntke, 'The 1990 all-German Campaign', in David Farrell and Shaun Bowler (eds.), *Election Strategies and Political Marketing* (London: Macmillan, 1993), p.128.
5. CDU, 1994, p.13
6. CDU, op.cit., p.27
7. Rainer Frenkel, *Die Zeit*, 9 Oct. 1994, p.48; *Der Spiegel*, 31 Oct. 1994, p.28; *Süddeutsche Zeitung*, 16 Sept. 1994.
8. CDU, op.cit., p.24
9. This was associated with a phone-bank, staffed principally by volunteers, who took calls from the public and, with the aid of computerised versions of the party's policy pronouncements, answered inquiries.
10. Genscher, Lambsdoff and Möllemann were all former ministers, and prominent members of the NRW FDP. The rivalry between Kinkel (from the Baden-Württemberg FDP) and Möllemann revealed itself at various times throughout *Superwahljahr*, and continued after the Bundestag election. Möllemann's critical attitude to Kinkel's leadership was a major reason for his being replaced as Land chairman at the end of 1994.
11. Boll and Poguntke, op.cit., p.138.
12. Boll and Poguntke, op.cit., p.140.
13. Klaus Schönbach and Holli A. Semetko, 'Medienberichtenstattung und Parteienwerbung im Bundestagwahlkampf 1990', *Media Perspektiven*, 7/1994, p.339.
14. Max Kaase, 'Is there personalization in politics? Candidates and voting behaviour in Germany', *International Political Science Review*, 15 (3), p.226.

REFERENCES

Boll, Bernhard and Poguntke, Thomas (1993), 'The 1990 all-German Campaign', in Farrell, David and Bowler, Shaun (eds.), *Election Strategies and Political Marketing* (London: Macmillan), pp.121–41.

CDU (1994), ''Deutschland erneuern – Zukunft sichern'. Bericht der Bundesgeschäftsstelle. Anlage zum Bericht des Bundesgeschäftsführers. 6. Parteitag der CDU Deutschlands, 28 Nov. 1994, Bonn. (no publisher).

Forschungsgruppe Wahlen (1994), 'Bundestagswahl 1994. Eine Analyse der Wahl zum 13. Deutschen Bundestag am 16.Oktober 1994', FGW-Bericht, No.76, Mannheim.

Hoffmann, Gunter (1994), 'Aus Furcht vor dem Volk', in *Die Zeit*, No.42, 14.10.1994, p.4.

Kaase, Max (1994), 'Is there Personalization in Politics? Candidates and Voting Behaviour in Germany', *International Political Science Review*, Vol.15, No.3, pp.211–30.

Mauser, Gary A.(1983), *Political Marketing. An Approach to Campaign Strategies* (New York: Praeger).

Reiser, Stefan (1994), 'Thematisierungsstrategien und Wahlkampfmanagement. Politik und Massenmedien im Wahlkampf', *Media Perspektiven*, 7/1994, pp.341–8.

Radunski, Peter (1980), *Wahlkämpfe. Wahlkampfführung als politische Kommunikation* (München: Olzog Verlag).

Sarcinelli, Ulrich (1987), *Symbolische Politik. Zur Bedeutung symbolischen Handelns in der Wahlkampfkommunikation* (Opladen: Westdeutscher Verlag).

Schönbach, Klaus und Semetko, Holli A. (1994), 'Medienberichterstattung und Parteienwerbung im Bundestagswahlkampf 1990', *Media Perspektiven*, 7/1994, pp.328–40.

Pointing the Way: The Electoral Transition from the Bonn Republic to the Berlin Republic

PETER PULZER

The 1994 Bundestag election exhibited features both of continuity and of change. Like the 1949 election (a bridge between the Weimar and Bonn political systems), the 1994 election can also be considered as transitional: between the old Bonn Republic and the new, post-unification, Berlin Republic. It did, though, confirm what previous Bundestag elections had established: that Germany can be governed only from the centre and only by coalition, that electoral contests are bipolar and that governments tend to get re-elected. The extent to which the post-unification party system differs from the 'old' Federal Republic is assessed. Despite the degree of continuity visible, it is likely that the party system will not be unaffected by post-unification pressures.

Elections serve many purposes, quite apart from the obvious ones. They exist, as we know, to produce a legislature that more or less reflects the state of public opinion, with the electoral system as a significant variable. In states with a parliamentary constitution they also exist to indicate the shape of the government, though the greater the number of parties, the less directly the voter can determine that particular outcome. One of the most interesting developments in the political conventions of the old Federal Republic was the way in which Bundestag elections increasingly became plebiscites about the composition of the executive. They never became exclusively that; West German democracy was always more than mere 'chancellor democracy' and West German parties – even the CDU in the heyday of Adenauer's dominance – were always more than 'associations for electing the Chancellor' (*Kanzlerwahlvereine*). But the trend in that direction was salutary. It educated German voters into considering the this-worldly consequences of the electoral act, a norm not always observed in the lifetime of the Weimar Republic. Two developments in particular helped to codify this convention. The first was the decision by the SPD in the 1961 election to accept the conventions of chancellor democracy by nominating its own chancellor candidate – a precedent that every opposition party has followed since then. The second was the decision by the SPD and FDP in 1972 to announce in advance that they would continue their coalition if the post-election parliamentary arithmetic permitted it – a convention also followed since then by all incumbent coalitions at the federal level and, more often than not, at the Land level as well.

One consequence of this change in conventions is that Article 67 of the Basic Law, prescribing the 'constructive vote of no confidence', so hotly debated in the Parliamentary Council of 1948–49 and seen at the time as the key to regime stability, has become almost redundant. It has been invoked only twice in 46 years; on the only occasion when it resulted in a change of government – in 1982, when the FDP switched its support from Helmut Schmidt to Helmut Kohl – the Federal Constitutional Court regarded such a change without an electoral mandate as so anomalous as to permit a premature dissolution. In other words, the notion that underlay the provisions of the Basic Law, namely, that legislative elections and government formation are conceptually and temporally separate procedures, has largely evaporated: a German election nowadays is, more than anything else, a plebiscite between government and alternative government.

That is, however, only one aspect of the electoral process. To think of an election primarily as the constituting event in the formation of a parliament or a government is to take a static view of elections: it is the snapshot definition of an election, which sees it as the expression of a momentary conjuncture of opinions and preferences. We know, of course, that this snapshot is not an isolated event. It is preceded by a campaign; voters vote in the knowledge of how the outgoing parliament and government have performed and with some assumptions about the quality of the forthcoming parliament and government; and a great many votes are cast out of habit and loyalty, largely independently of what is said in the campaign or how the outgoing parliament and government performed. In spite of these factors, the single event is apt to be analysed statically.

There is, however, another aspect to an election. Elections, at any rate in a stable democratic state, are part of a dynamic process. They happen at regular intervals; from one election to the next there is a large overlap in participating politicians, parties and voters. Elections enable us to trace trendlines, fluctuations, continuities and upheavals. Long ago the analysts of the Michigan school taught us to distinguish between normal, critical and reinstating elections.[1] Tools of this kind enable us to see any given election in perspective. In particular, it can tell us a great deal about its predecessor. The 1992 election in Britain went some way towards answering the question whether the Conservative hegemony of the 1980s was dependent on one particular leader or one specific ideological identification. The 1996 elections in the United States will help us to know whether it was Clinton's victory in 1992 – only the second Democratic presidential win since 1964 – or the Republican landslide of 1994 – the first since 1928 – that is most in need of explanation.

So it is with the Bundestag election of 1994. It puts the 1990 election, the first for a united Germany, into perspective. Since it resulted, however narrowly, in the re-election of Helmut Kohl's coalition, the outcome is most obviously a symptom of continuity. It was Kohl's fourth successive election victory, making him, with Felipe Gonzalez of Spain, the longest serving head of government in Europe. If he serves out his fourth full term until 1996 he will have comfortably outlasted Adenauer's tenure of 13 years and be not far short of Bismarck's 19-year record. Yet, all these continuities notwithstanding, there are also indications of transformation. It is clearer in 1994 than it was at the time that the 1990 election was an election of transition, not so much because of the emotionally charged atmosphere in which it took place, but because it was neither the last election of the Bonn Republic, nor the first of the Berlin Republic. In important ways it resembled that of 1949, which looked back to Weimar as well as looking forward to Bonn.[2]

With nine parties elected to the first Bundestag, there were reasons for thinking that the multi-party spectrum of Weimar and, indeed, the Empire, even though modified, would remain a feature of German politics. The electoral geography of the late 1940s suggested that regional traditions, sub-cultures and *milieux* had survived the 12 years of the Third Reich fairly intact, or at any rate had been effectively resuscitated. As against that the main new force in German politics, the CDU, emerged as the biggest single party, admittedly with only 31 per cent of the vote. But the fact that its nominee, Konrad Adenauer, became the first Federal Chancellor meant that it was in a good position to assume the hegemonial position it was later to occupy. Moreover, 1949 was not an electoral year zero for the Western Länder. In all of them citizens had participated in at least two Land-wide elections in 1946 or 1947, which had made it possible to monitor the potential of the new parties. The 1949 election was Janus-like. The two main parties, SPD and CDU/CSU, gained 60 per cent between them, more than any two parties had ever gained in German electoral history, but well below the 90–91 per cent they were to achieve in the 1970s. The fragmentation of the centre-right, always a feature of the German party scene, but particularly conspicuous in 1928–30, was reduced, but not ended. The KPD, still a significant force in the Western Länder immediately after the war, was shrinking and would in the course of time have been reduced to negligible proportions even if it had not been banned under Article 21(2) of the Basic Law. But for the moment it was still there and at the end of

1950 it held seats in over half the Western Landtage. The 1990 election, too, was Janus-like, with one face towards Bonn and the other towards Berlin, but it is only the election of 1994 – and perhaps also that of 1998 – that makes that clear. In many respects even the 1994 election is marked more by continuity than by a break in convention. It confirmed four rules about German politics that had been established before unification: Germany can be governed only from the political centre; Germany can be governed only by coalition; electoral contests are bi-polar; federal governments are re-elected.[3] Perhaps a word should be said in support of these propositions.

The first, that Germany can be governed only from the centre, is to a large degree dependent on the second. Since 1957 there have been only two parties in the ruling coalition and for all but seven of those 37 years one of the coalition partners has been the FDP. Extreme parties are, by definition, excluded from coalition participation and *de facto* from the Bundestag – at any rate if one counts the Greens of the 1980s as non-extremist and, more doubtfully, the post-1989 PDS. Even at the Land level co-operation with extremist parties is taboo. The grand coalition in Baden-Württemberg, in office since 1992, came into existence through the need to marginalise the Republicans. If the NPD had been elected to the Bundestag in 1969, instead of winning only 4.3 per cent, the continuation of the federal great coalition would have been unavoidable. The passive support of the PDS for the minority SPD–Green government in Sachsen-Anhalt, following the 1994 Landtag election, has turned out to be an exception. In Thüringen and Mecklenburg-Vorpommern, where there are also parliamentary majorities for the SPD and PDS following the 1994 Landtag elections, grand coalitions are in office. The taboo against extremism is probably stronger than in any other continental European state. One has only to consider the pivotal position of the Front National, the FPÖ and the ex-MSI at the regional level in France, Austria and Italy, and the participation of the PCF and the Allianza Nazionale in national governments in France and Italy. The knowledge that extremist parties are excluded from government and that a vote for them is therefore wasted, except as a form of protest, may well influence voter choice and further bunch the German party spectrum towards the centre.

Bipolar electoral contests are also a consequence of the conventions of chancellor democracy. In this respect they reflect the wishes of politicians more than of voters. The first and, in many ways, most skilful practitioner of chancellor democracy, Konrad Adenauer, was determined to isolate the SPD and keep it in opposition; his election campaigns of 1953, 1957 and 1961 were therefore conducted not only on behalf of himself, but against the SPD. The degree of polarisation in later elections has fluctuated, but it has never been absent. It has, if anything, been enhanced by the post-1972 convention of declaring coalition strategies in advance. There is, nevertheless, something paradoxical about this polarised campaigning. It does not necessarily correspond with public preferences: most German citizens prefer consensus to conflict, as repeated opinion surveys have shown. Though there is no longer a majority for grand coalitions, as there was in the 1960s, these retain considerable support. Nor does this polarisation correspond with the way policy is made. Most legislation emerges by consensus, partly because that is the way the Bundestag works, with an emphasis on attention to detail in committees rather than rhetorical battles in floor debates, partly also because dissonant majorities in the Bundestag and Bundesrat, which have been the norm during the 1970s and 1990s, impose cross-party conciliation.

Lastly, there is the lack of governmental alternation arising out of elections. No West German or all-German government has so far lost an election. The changes of government that have occurred have arisen out of party re-alignment and, in two cases out of three, in mid-term. The 1966 change from the CDU–FDP government to the grand coalition came about when the FDP resigned from the Erhard government. After the 1969 election the grand coalition could easily have remained in office, but the SPD, who had been the junior partner in the grand coalition, preferred to govern with the FDP. This was the first genuine *Machtwechsel*, but, though it followed the election, it was not the necessary outcome of it. Finally, the second *Machtwechsel* of 1982 also took place because of a change of partner by the FDP. The electoral endorsement of this was, as we have seen, retrospective. Even these *Machtwechsel* were not true alternations. In each instance one of the partners in the outgoing government remained in office in the succeeding one. That means that governmental alternations correspond even less with policy revolutions than they do in other countries with parliamentary constitutions. Promises of policy change (*Wende*) are not always delivered; the greatest policy changes may be a mid-term response to an unanticipated external impulse. Indeed, paradoxically, the two main alternations of power have served to endorse policy changes initiated by their predecessors. The Brandt–Scheel government of 1969–74 has gone down in history for its achievement of *Ostpolitik* and its domestic reformist euphoria. But *Ostpolitik*, in the sense of exploring a new relationship with the GDR and the other states of the Communist bloc, was initiated by the grand coalition, in which Brandt was Foreign Minister; in terms of domestic reforms, the grand coalition actually achieved more than the Brandt government, largely thanks to Gustav Heinemann of the SPD at the Ministry of Justice; in economic policy the trend towards greater state intervention, counter-cyclical macro-economic steering and the mild corporatism of Concerted Action were also initiated under the grand coalition by Karl Schiller of the SPD as Minister for the Economy. These initiatives might well not have been completed but for the *Machtwechsel*, but the real *Wende* came in 1966. The second significant *Wende* came in 1974, when Helmut Schmidt succeeded Brandt as Chancellor. The party composition of the 'social–liberal' coalition was unchanged, but the policy direction was not. In response to the oil shock, but also to domestically generated inflationary pressures, Schmidt pursued a tight money policy, giving priority to currency stability over both full employment and welfare expansion. In defence policy he responded to Soviet missile deployment with the twin-track decision of 1979, which entailed the installation of cruise and Pershing missiles in western Europe. Once more the *Machtwechsel* of 1982 was an endorsement of the preceding government's *Wende*, the SPD–FDP coalition having broken up over divisions within the SPD on both economic and defence policy; indeed, the *Machtwechsel* was, as in 1969, the guarantee of policy continuity.

Unification certainly brought about a change in the external environment of German politics. Did coalition continuity hide another policy *Wende*? The answer must be: only to a limited extent. The need to rehabilitate the economy of the GDR has brought about a greater role for the state, through higher taxes, higher transfer payments and a shift of influence and authority from the Länder to the federation. The autonomy of the major social actors, which was a guiding principle of the old-style social market economy, had to be, if not suspended, considerably modified. It culminated in the deal between government, opposition, Länder and interest groups that produced the Solidarity Pact of March 1993 – a 'renaissance of corporatism'.[4] The Solidarity Pact was an emergency measure and its provisions are meant to have a time limit. Since its terms were agreed by the SPD opposition, an SPD victory would have brought about little change, at any rate in this central policy area: it would have been another *Machtwechsel* without *Wende*.

Lastly, what of the post-unification party system? How, if at all, do the alignments of the Berlin Republic differ from those of the Bonn Republic? The 1990 election was certainly less innovative than that of 1949. In 1949 there were two major new actors: the CDU and the FDP. The most significant characteristic of the 1990 election was the ease with which the established west German party system was translated to the former GDR; 79 per cent of east German voters voted for the CDU, SPD or FDP. The only new actors of any significance were the PDS, the successor party of the Communist SED, with 11.1 per cent, and the coalition of civil rights groups, Bündnis 90, with 5.3 per cent. In some respects the 1994 results confirm this post-unification alignment, in others they have modified them. The share of the three main Bonn parties in the new Länder is slightly down at 73.5 per cent. This is due entirely to the decline of the FDP (from 12.9 to 3.5 per cent); the two *Volksparteien* have improved their joint share from 66.1 per cent to 69 per cent. It might, however, be best to analyse the outcome party by party.

CDU/CSU

The Union parties secured 41.4 per cent of the vote, their worst result since 1949. However, in relation to the performance of other European Christian Democratic parties, this result is little short of a triumph. In Austria, Belgium and the Netherlands, where Christian Democrats were for long the dominant parties, they have dropped below 30 per cent; in Italy they have virtually disappeared and in France completely so. The German achievement is all the more remarkable, since the new Länder are structurally most inhospitable to Christian Democracy: there are few Catholics and not all that many observant Protestants; few self-employed in industry and virtually none in agriculture. In fact the CDU has compensated for this unpromising social structure by becoming the party of blue-collar workers, especially in the southern Länder of Sachsen and Thüringen. To what extent the CDU's success is a reflection of the 'Kohl factor', and what will happen to the CDU once the 'unification Chancellor' has stepped down, remains to be seen. But with the CDU supplying three of the five eastern Land premiers, the party looks reasonably well implanted in the former GDR.

SPD

The SPD has, for the fourth time since 1982, failed to displace the CDU as the governing party, but it has stopped the rot. Having lost votes in 1983, 1987 and 1990, it has made something of a recovery. Above all, it has made good some of its deficit in the eastern Länder. It has halved the gap between its eastern and western performance from 11.4 per cent in 1990 to 6.0 per cent, while the CDU has widened its gap from 2.5 per cent to 4.6 per cent. As a result of the Landtag elections of 1994 it has an absolute majority in Brandenburg and participates in the government of three of the other four Länder. Though still well below the level of its peak performance in the 1970s – indeed, polling scarcely better than it did in 1912 – it has, like the CDU, done well in international comparison. With 36.4 per cent it is the fourth strongest Social Democratic party in Europe, ranking after those of Sweden and Spain and just behind that of Norway.

FDP

The Free Democrats, experienced in the art of survival, survived once more, though only after some alarms. The FDP's 6.9 per cent share of the vote is better only than its cliff-hanging share of 5.8 per cent in 1969. Exit polls showed that many of the votes cast for it were tactical and that it seems to serve no purpose other than that of ensuring a parliamentary majority for Helmut Kohl. Under the leadership of Klaus Kinkel it lacks both the distinctive policy profile and the distinguished personalities that marked its role under the leadership of Otto Graf Lambsdorff, Hans-Dietrich Genscher and Walter Scheel. That emerged most clearly in its losses in the eastern Länder. Where it had been 2.3 per cent ahead of its western vote in 1990 on the strength of the Genscher bonus, it was now 4.2 per cent behind.

Alliance 90/Greens

Within this uneasy alliance the fortunes of 1990 were reversed. Whereas in 1990 the Greens were punished for their scepticism *vis-à-vis* unification, they are now firmly re-established as a component of the German party system. Having disposed of their 'fundamentalist' radical wing, they are now, in their own eyes at least, ready for participation in coalition government at the federal as well as the Land level. They have travelled a long way since the early 1980s, when they saw themselves primarily as an anti-system movement, determined to avoid an establishment embrace. Bündnis 90, in the eastern Länder, on the other hand, remains a single-issue group within the party that concentrates on settling scores with the regime of the former GDR. As the political agenda has moved on to other issues, this is a wasting asset. With only 3.8 per cent in the eastern Länder, Bündnis 90 is wholly dependent on the western Greens' coat-tails.

PDS

The recovery of the semi-reformed successor party of the SED is probably the feature of this election that fewest would have forecast in 1990. Having dropped from 16.4 per cent at the Volkskammer election of March 1990 to 11.1 per cent at the Bundestag election of December 1990, it seemed doomed to further decline. Though its paid-up membership is senescent, its electoral following is spread evenly through the various age-groups. The municipal elections in Brandenburg in December 1993 gave the first warning that a sizeable protest vote was accumulating in the eastern Länder and that this did not consist exclusively of those who were 'unification losers' in the material sense. The PDS remains overwhelmingly a party of the eastern Länder, having gained 19.8 per cent there, as opposed to 1.0 per cent in the west. Its support is sufficiently concentrated for it to benefit from the provision in the electoral law that entitles a party to proportional representation if it wins three constituencies outright even though it fails to clear the five per cent hurdle nationally. However, the PDS's votes in the west should not be ignored. One per cent of the eastern vote equals 86,000 votes; one per cent of the western vote equals 385,000 votes. Two out of every 11 PDS votes came from the west, as did five of its 30 seats. Support for the PDS in the western Länder may be insignificant in terms of total western votes, but not in terms of total PDS votes.

Republicans

After the mid-term gains by the far right in both Landtag and municipal elections, the Republicans reverted to the insignificant totals they had secured in 1990 – 1.9 per cent, compared with 2.1 per cent. As periodic surges have shown, there is clearly a far right potential in Germany, though it is lower than in France, Italy or Austria. But it is also unstable and its parties have never succeeded in making a breakthrough at 'first-order' elections.

What conclusions can one draw from the 1994 election about the dynamics of German electoral behaviour and of the party system? There is evidence for both stability and movement. Taking Germany as a whole, we can see it as a restabilising election. The party fragmentation that seemed to threaten in 1992 and 1993, with a grand coalition as the most likely outcome, did not happen. Nor was there much evidence for the *Politikverdrossenheit* that so many observers claimed to detect in those years. The turn-out was higher than in 1990 (79 per cent, compared with 77.8 per cent) and the share of the two main parties almost unchanged (77.8 per cent, compared with 77.3 per cent). The slide in the major parties' share of the total electorate, a continuous trend since 1976, has been reversed.

However, though the global picture is one of re-stabilisation, there has been greater regionalisation in the strengths of individual parties. The western Länder now have a four-party system (CDU–CSU, SPD, FDP, Greens) and the eastern Länder a three-party system (CDU, SPD, PDS). There are only two truly national parties. In the western Länder continuity from the Bonn Republic to the Berlin Republic has bordered on the amazing.

It is in the eastern Länder that volatility is greater, though even there party loyalties are stable compared with other states of the former Communist bloc. For every party except the SPD the gap between eastern

TABLE 1

TURN-OUT AND MAJOR PARTY SHARES IN BUNDESTAG ELECTIONS 1972–1994

	Turn-out	CDU–CSU+SPD	CDU–CSU+SPD
	%	% of votes cast	% of electorate
		(western Länder only)	
1972	91.1	90.7	82.6
1976	90.7	91.2	82.7
1980	88.6	87.4	77.4
1983	89.1	87.0	77.5
1987	84.3	81.3	68.5
1990	78.6	80.0	62.9
1994	80.5	79.6	64.1
		(all Länder)	
1990	77.8	77.3	60.2
1994	79.0	77.8	61.5

TABLE 2

PARTY STRENGTHS IN WESTERN LÄNDER (%)

	1987	1994	Difference
CDU/CSU	44.3	42.1	-2.2
SPD	37.0	37.5	+0.5
FDP	9.1	7.7	-1.4
Greens	8.3	7.9	-0.4

and western shares has widened. One major effect of this regional diversity is that the Bundesrat is more difficult to manage. The 16 Länder have five SPD governments, one CDU, one CSU, four grand coalitions, one SPD–FDP coalition, one 'traffic light' coalition, two SPD–Green coalitions and one SPD–Stattpartei coalition. There is no precedent for this kaleidoscope, but it is likely to be the pattern of the future.

The Berlin Republic has inherited the institutions of the Bonn Republic and, with them, its party structure. German unification was much less of a trauma and an upheaval than the post-war division of Germany and the experiment of creating the Federal Republic. The institutions that were transferred to the whole of Germany in 1990 under Article 23 of the Basic Law were tried and tested, and enjoyed popular legitimacy in the way that no previous German system of government had done. Nevertheless, the new demands and policy agenda that unification have brought are beginning to affect the way these institutions work and the parties are not exempt from these pressures.

NOTES

1. Philip E. Converse, 'The Concept of a Normal Vote', Philip Converse *et al.*, 'Stability and Change in 1960: A Reinstating Election', in Angus Campbell *et al.*, *Elections and the Political Order* (New York: Wiley, 1966); V.O. Key Jnr., 'A Theory of Critical Elections', *Journal of Politics*, Feb. 1955.
2. Jürgen W. Falter, 'Kontinuität und Neubeginn. Die Bundestagswahl 1949 zwischen Weimar und Bonn', *Politische Vierteljahresschrift*, 22 (1981), p.3.
3. See Peter Pulzer, 'The West German Federal Election of 25 January 1987', *Electoral Studies*, Aug.1987.
4. Razeen Sally and Douglas Webber, 'The German Solidarity Pact', *German Politics*, Vol.3, No.1 (April 1994), p.39.

Postscript: The Land Elections in Hessen, Nordrhein-Westfalen and Bremen

SIMON GREEN

The Länder elections in the early months of 1995 proved a first test for the parties and for the party system as it had emerged from 'Superwahljahr 1994'. The FDP had retained its representation in the Hessen legislature but failed badly in the Nordrhein-Westfalen and Bremen elections. Bündnis 90/Die Grünen proved to be the 'winners' in all three elections, continuing a coalition with the SPD in Hessen and forcing the creation of such a coalition in Nordrhein-Westfalen. In Bremen, a new 'party' (Arbeit für Bremen) seemed to have imitated the Statt-partei success in Hamburg in 1993, as a local breakaway party winning seats at its first election. Low turnout reflected the satiation of voters with elections through 1994–95.

Introduction

With the Federal election on 16 October 1994, along with Land elections in the Saarland, Mecklenburg Vorpommern and in Thüringen, *Superwahljahr* reached its climax. However, parties and voters were given little chance of respite after the plethora of electoral campaigns that characterised 1994 before the election bandwagon moved on again for three important regional elections.

The elections in Hessen in February, and in Nordrhein-Westfalen and Bremen in May, were of significance for all the main parties involved. The CDU, having emerged as winner of the Bundestag election, aimed to consolidate its success with good results in these three Länder, all of which are traditional SPD strongholds. The SPD, relieved by its Federal result, was keen to bolster its regional basis in its attempt to influence national politics through its predominance in the Bundesrat. Bündnis 90/Die Grünen (hereafter referred to as Die Grünen) had re-entered the Bundestag in 1994 after a four-year absence and hoped to continue its run of good results, while there was also the danger of extremist parties entering the respective state legislatures, with the extreme German People's Union (DVU) even defending its representation in the Bremen Bürgerschaft.

The FDP's position, however, was considerably more precarious.

Between 1993 and 1994, it had unsuccessfully contested nine Land elections, as well as the European election, and there was even considerable doubt as to whether the FDP would pass the five per cent hurdle in the Bundestag election. In the event, it did, but only by virtue of lent votes of CDU supporters, which did nothing to dispel the party's image of a lackey of the CDU. These three elections would thus be paramount in its efforts to reassert its credibility as an independent force in post-unification Germany.

The Hessen Land Election of 19 February 1995

The Land election in Hessen was the first test of public opinion since October's federal election, and provided an opportunity for the CDU to recapture from the SPD and Die Grünen a state in which it had formed a coalition with the FDP from 1987 to 1991. The campaign was rather dull, with no outstanding personalities, issues or differences between the two main parties. Such a lack of political debate clearly failed to motivate the electorate to vote, as the lowest turnout figures since 1950 testify. The CDU, under Federal Interior Minister Manfred Kanther, a well-known law-and-order hardliner, managed to regain its position as largest party in Hessen, but was unable to dislodge the incumbent SPD–Die Grünen coalition under Minister-President Hans Eichel, which had been in power since 1991. However, the SPD itself polled a very poor result, at 38.0 per cent its worst ever, and it lost heavily in urban areas such as Frankfurt, Offenbach and Kassel. Its continued position in government was thus only assured by the exceptionally good result of Die Grünen, who at 11.2 per cent polled their best ever result in a *Flächenstaat*, that is, in a non-city state. The FDP, with 7.4 per cent, managed to break its devastating run of electoral defeats in the nine previous Land elections, but remains in opposition with the CDU.

While the FDP's return to the Wiesbaden assembly was an undoubted success, the party was to be granted no more than temporary relief from its troubles. In Hessen particularly, the FDP benefited from a dual vote electoral system identical to that at federal level, thereby allowing voters to 'split' their votes. The analysis of the Forschungsgruppe Wahlen showed that, although the FDP received 7.4 per cent of second votes, only 4.7 per cent of first votes were cast in its favour; moreover, 42 per cent of its second voters expressed a preference for the CDU.[1] These figures reflect the phenomenon of 'lent votes' from habitual CDU-voters the FDP experienced at the October Bundestag election, as well as the FDP's shrinking *Stammwählerschaft*.

The Nordrhein-Westfalen Election of 14 May 1995

The ominous signs for the FDP set by the Hessen election came to bear fully in the elections in Bremen and Nordrhein-Westfalen. Especially the latter election was seen as a watershed in the FDP's medium-term fortunes: as well as being Germany's most populous state, it has the highest FDP membership levels of any state, and has traditionally produced a string of prominent liberal politicians, including ex-Foreign Minister Hans-Dietrich Genscher, ex-Economics Minister Otto Graf Lambsdorff and former Federal President Walter Scheel.

The election campaign itself was rather lacklustre and largely devoid of content, with 75 per cent of all voters expecting the SPD to win, and 50 per cent predicting that the popular SPD Minister-President since 1979, Johannes Rau, would be returned with an absolute majority.[2] The result, however, proved to be a shock for both the SPD and the FDP.

The SPD's result was disappointing: it narrowly missed its aim of a fourth consecutive absolute majority, and now finds itself having to go into coalition with Die Grünen in order to stay in power. Although the SPD sustained losses in all geographic areas, it suffered most from mobilisation problems and very low levels of turnout (around 55 per cent) in the industrial cities of the Ruhr, traditionally its bedrock of support; in total, it lost almost half a million votes to the growing reservoir of non-voters. Its poor result, moreover, is a personal blow to Rau, who during the campaign had publicly stated his distaste for a coalition by declaring his intention to 'govern, not negotiate', especially not with Die Grünen.

The CDU, which had set itself the target of 40 per cent + x, found its support had even shown a slight increase. It had, however, no realistic chance of replacing Rau, as the SPD's competence ratings in all areas except law and order were higher, and the CDU's leading candidate, Helmut Linssen, was widely unknown, even among his own party.

By contrast, the election result for the FDP was nothing short of disastrous. Unlike the federal electoral system, Nordrhein-Westfalen operates a single vote system based on constituencies, which does not permit the 'split-ticket' strategy which has so often benefited the party. Although the result is proportional, the FDP has to rely especially heavily on its core voters. In its attempt to present a stronger profile, the regional party had in December 1994 opted for a change of leadership. It thus replaced the ambitious Jürgen Möllemann, who had resigned as Federal Economics Minister as a result of a sleaze-like scandal in January 1993, with the untainted, but unknown, Joachim Schultz-Tornau as its chairman. However, such a move proved to be to no avail: the FDP's failure to commit itself to one coalition partner and to present a coherent image at Land level, combined with voters' expectations of a Land government without FDP involvement sufficed to remove the party from the Düsseldorf legislature for only the second time in the state's history.

Die Grünen, however, were the real winners of the election. Fresh from their strong showing in the Hessen election, they doubled their share of the vote, scoring especially highly in university cities and among first-time voters. Indeed, in one constituency in central Köln, Die Grünen took 29.8 per cent of the vote.

The Bremen Election of 14 May 1995

The northern German city state of Bremen is, even more so than Nordrhein-Westfalen, traditionally an SPD stronghold. The Land election, originally scheduled for autumn of this year, was brought forward when the so-called 'traffic light coalition' of SPD, FDP and Die Grünen collapsed over an internal dispute in January. Plagued by unemployment and financial problems of the public purse, the election was hotly contested, not only by the major parties, but also by smaller parties on the fringes of the political spectrum.

The results (Table 3) are even more disappointing for the SPD than those in Nordrhein-Westfalen. For the party which consistently between 1971 and 1991 ruled alone in Bremen, and which in 1987 had still polled over 50 per cent, a slump to one-third of cast votes, only just ahead of the CDU, was a bitter rebuke by the voters. The Forschungsgruppe Wahlen's analysis showed the SPD's substantial losses to be due to its perceived lack of competence in all areas and to internal strife in the party, which had caused a group of right-wing party members to form the Arbeit für Bremen (AFB) citizens' group in January.[3] This group had campaigned on a programme of vigorous restructuring of public finances, with evident success: almost half of its voters came from the SPD, with another 20 per cent coming from both the FDP and CDU. As a result of the election, the incumbent ruling mayor, Klaus Wedemeier (SPD), resigned, and has been replaced by Henning Scherf, previously Senator for Education.

The CDU's result was a resounding success for its candidate, local businessman Ulrich Nölle. It saw its share of the vote rise to its third-highest ever, and even came close to overtaking the SPD, a result of its problem-solving competence in all major policy areas. Die Grünen saw their share of the vote rise again, a reflection of the social structure of the Bremen electorate, which, as a city with a large university, clearly favours them.

The FDP's failure to re-enter the Bürgerschaft came on top of the disastrous result in Nordrhein-Westfalen. Hampered by a single-vote system of proportional representation, the party slumped to its lowest result ever in Bremen. It lost heavily to the CDU and the AFB, the latter of which presented a viable alternative, untainted by involvement in the traffic-light coalition, for the secular middle-class voters upon which the FDP depends so much.

Of the smaller parties contesting the election, much attention was focused on the performance of the reformed ex-Communists, the Party of Democratic Socialism (PDS). In its attempts to develop beyond a party for disgruntled former GDR apparatchiks, the PDS had targeted Bremen for its expansion into the old Länder, in which it considered itself to have good chances, due to the high proportion of younger voters in the city state. Nonetheless, its result of 2.4 per cent, below its showing in that state in the 1994 Bundestag election, was a serious blow, as there are no other obvious states in the west where it might succeed in gaining a foothold.

On the other side of the political spectrum, there were worries that the extreme right wing German People's Union (DVU) would manage to secure representation for the third time after 1987 and 1991. Indeed, although their result was poor compared to 1991, the party missed representation by a mere 186 votes, due to a quirk in the Bremen electoral law, which allows parties to be represented if they poll 5 per cent in either Bremen or the attached city of Bremerhaven, a DVU stronghold.[4] The party's permanent exclusion from the Bürgerschaft can thus not be guaranteed.

Consequences of the Elections

Overall, the results for the CDU were good. Its vote held up in traditional SPD areas, and it has formed a Grand Coalition with the SPD in Bremen as well as regaining its status as largest party in Hessen. The SPD, although considerably weakened in areas where it should have been romping home, can continue to rule in Hessen and Nordrhein-Westfalen thanks to the strength of Die Grünen.

However, it was Die Grünen who enjoyed the greatest success, with substantial gains in all three elections. In a climate of falling turnout, Die Grünen benefited strongly from its highly motivated electorate: in both Nordrhein-Westfalen and Bremen, they were the only party to increase their absolute number of votes. Their transformation from citizens' movement to established party now seems complete, and they have, moreover, advanced into the position previously held by the FDP, that of third largest party nationally. The party is currently represented in 11 Land parliaments, as well as being in coalition with the SPD in three. This sends an unmistakable message, backed by senior SPD figures such as Gerhard Schröder and Oskar Lafontaine, to the party chairman, Rudolf Scharping, that the possibility of such a coalition at federal level can no longer be discounted. Indeed, the SPD–Die Grünen coalition in Nordrhein-Westfalen has been heralded as a dry run for a possible Bonn coalition.

The success of Die Grünen has also resulted in the possibility of

CDU–Die Grünen coalitions being mooted by senior CDU politicians, such as Heiner Geißler, the deputy parliamentary leader in the Bundestag. Although the first such coalitions have appeared at local (*Kommunal*) level following local elections in Nordrhein-Westfalen in October 1994 in the town of Mülheim an der Ruhr, the realistic chance of such an alliance forming at Land level must, in the short term, remain small. Moreover, at federal level, such a development can be discounted.

In stark contrast to Die Grünen's success stands the FDP's continued electoral misery. Following the latest defeats, it retains representation in only five out of 16 Land legislatures, as well as involvement in only one Land government. The party has thus lost its position as the linchpin of the party system. Devoid of programmatic identity, lacking in dynamic leaders of the calibre of ex-Foreign Minister Hans-Dietrich Genscher, robbed of a regional basis through repeated failure at the polls, the FDP is being squeezed simultaneously by the CDU, the SPD and even by Die Grünen. Once out of a Landtag, it is moreover very difficult to return, and whereas the FDP has managed to achieve this in individual states throughout its existence, it has never before been faced with this problem on such a wide scale. The renewed failure of the FDP in critical states where it needed to gain representation to bolster its position casts a shadow over the governing coalition in Bonn, where the CDU is effectively attached to a dying party. Increasingly, thus, the FDP's role is seen solely as a '*Mehrheitsbeschaffer*' at federal level, as that of a kingmaker, a role which it cannot hope to exercise successfully in the long run. Following these latest setbacks, the FDP chairman, Klaus Kinkel, resigned, and has been replaced by the relatively unknown Wolfgang Gerhardt, the chairman of the Hessen regional party.

On a lesser note, turnout continues to be low in all three states. In Hessen and Nordrhein-Westfalen turnout sank to its lowest-ever level, while in Bremen it was the second-lowest recorded. Such trends may be a reflection of several factors, such as *Wahlmüdigkeit* on the part of the electorate after fifteen months of almost constant campaigning, the fact that in Nordrhein-Westfalen the SPD was widely expected to win, or a more widely felt *Politikverdrossenheit* among the population. More importantly, they reflect the growing reservoir of votes which the established parties are failing to mobilise. The possibilities for other parties to make an impact, such as the AFB in Bremen, is thus increased.

Conclusions

For the FDP, its success in Hessen may well turn out to have been a Pyrrhic victory. Its immediate future looks bleak, with no sign of a light at the end of the tunnel: of the upcoming Land elections, Baden-Württemberg and Rheinland-Pfulz early next year stand out as of especial importance: the former is arguably the FDP's *Stammland*, and the latter is the last state where the FDP is still in government. Were the FDP to collapse to under five per cent here as well, a radical reorientation towards the national-conservative right, a foretaste of which was offered at the party's traditional *Dreikönigstreffen* in January in Stuttgart, may become more plausible.

On the national stage, while the Bonn coalition looks secure for the time being, the CDU is being forced to consider alternatives for the future. The weakness of the CDU's junior coalition partner has prompted Edmund Stoiber, the Bavarian Minister-President, to urge Chancellor Kohl to reconsider his decision not to run as Chancellor candidate in the 1998 election, as well as advising the CDU to aim for an absolute majority.[5] Whatever course is taken, it is clear that the voters in Hessen, Nordrhein-Westfalen and Bremen have dealt the parties some interesting cards to play in the near future.

NOTES

1. *Süddeutsche Zeitung*, 21 Feb. 1995.
2. Konrad-Adenauer-Stiftung, *Das Wahlergebnis der Landtagswahl in Nordrhein-Westfalen vom 14. Mai 1995 und seine wesentlichen Bestimmungsgründe*, Sankt Augustin.
3. *Süddeutsche Zeitung*, 16 May 1995.
4. By vitue of this anomaly, the DVU managed to gain representation in the *Bürgerschaft* in 1987, even though it polled only 3.4% throughout the state.
5. *Frankfurter Rundschau*, 22 May 1995.

APPENDIX

'SUPERWAHLJAHR' 1994: KEY DATES

13 March	Niedersachsen Land election.
20 March	Local elections, Schleswig-Holstein.
22 March	Collapse of 'traffic-light' coalition in Brandenburg.
23 May	Election of Roman Herzog as Federal President.
3 June	FDP party congress at Rostock confirms decision taken by party Praesidium (on 11 April) and party Executive (on 2 May) to seek to continue the coalition with the Christian Democrats after the Bundestag election.
12 June	Elections to European Parliament; local elections in Thüringen, Sachsen, Sachsen-Anhalt, Mecklenburg-Vorpommern, Baden-Württemberg, Saarland and Rheinland-Pfalz.
26 June	Sachsen-Anhalt Land election.
11 September	Brandenburg and Sachsen Land elections.
25 September	Bayern Land election.
16 October	Bundestag election; Saarland, Thüringen and Mecklenburg-Vorpommern Land elections; Nordrhein-Westfalen local elections.
10 November	Newly elected Bundestag meets.
15 November	Helmut Kohl re-relected as Federal Chancellor with 338 votes of 671.
17 November	New cabinet appointed.

ELECTION RESULTS 1994*

*Note: vote percentages are second votes where applicable.

TABLE 1

ELECTION TO THE NIEDERSACHSEN LAND PARLIAMENT 1994 AND 1990

Party	Election 13/3/1994		Election 13/5/1990	
	%	Seats	%	Seats
CDU	34.6	67	42.0	67
SPD	44.3	81	44.2	71
FDP	4.4	–	6.0	9
Bündnis 90/	7.4	13	5.0	8
Die Grünen[1]				
Others	7.5	–	2.3	–
Total seats		161		155
Turnout	73.8		74.6	

Note: 1. In 1990, Die Grünen.

TABLE 2

ELECTION TO THE EUROPEAN PARLIAMENT 1994 AND 1989

Party	Election 12/6/1994		Election 18/6/1990	
	%	Seats	%	Seats
CDU/CSU	38.8	47	37.7	31
SPD	32.2	40	37.3	30
FDP	4.1	–	5.6	4
Bündnis 90/	10.1	12	8.4	7
Die Grünen[1]				
PDS[2]	4.7	–	–	–
Republikaner	3.9	–	7.1	6
Others	6.3	–	3.7	–
Total seats		99		78[3]
Turnout	60.1		62.3	

Notes: 1. In 1989, Die Grünen.
2. The PDS did not exist in 1989, so did not contest that election.
3. In addition, four members of the European Parliament were sent by the Berlin Land Legislature.

TABLE 3

ELECTION TO THE SACHSEN-ANHALT LAND PARLIAMENT 1994 AND 1990

Party	Election 26/6/1994		Election 14/10/1990	
	%	Seats	%	Seats
CDU	34.4	37	39.0	48
SPD	34.0	36	26.0	27
FDP	3.6	–	13.5	14
Bündnis 90/	5.1	5	5.3	5
Die Grünen[1]				
PDS	19.9	21	12.0	12
Others	3.1	–	4.2	–
Total seats		99		106
Turnout	54.9		65.1	

Note: 1. In 1990: Grüne Liste/Neues Forum.

TABLE 4

ELECTION TO THE BRANDENBURG LAND PARLIAMENT 1994 AND 1990

Party	Election 11/9/1994		Election 14/10/1990	
	%	Seats	%	Seats
CDU	18.7	18	29.5	27
SPD	54.1	52	38.2	36
FDP	2.2	–	6.6	6
Bündnis 90/	2.1	–	9.2	6
Die Grünen[1]				
PDS	18.7	18	13.4	13
Others	3.3	–	3.1	–
Total seats		88		88
Turnout	56.1		67.4	

Note: 1. In 1990: Bündnis 90 6.4 per cent; Die Grünen 2.8 per cent. The six seats were won by Bündnis 90.

TABLE 5

ELECTION TO THE SACHSEN LAND PARLIAMENT 1994 AND 1990

Party	Election 11/9/1994		Election 14/10/1990	
	%	Seats	%	Seats
CDU	58.1	77	54.4	92
SPD	16.6	22	19.1	32
FDP	1.7	–	5.3	9
Bündnis 90/	4.1	–	5.6	10
Die Grünen[1]				
PDS	16.5	21	10.2	17
Others	3.0	–	5.4	–
Total seats		120		160
Turnout	58.4		73.5	

Note: 1. In 1990, as Neues Forum/Bündnis 90/Die Grünen.

TABLE 6

ELECTION TO THE BAYERN LAND PARLIAMENT 1994 AND 1990

Party	Election 25/9/1994		Election 14/10/1990	
	%	Seats	%	Seats
CSU	52.8	120	54.9	127
SPD	30.1	70	26.0	58
FDP	2.8	–	5.2	7
Bündnis 90/	6.1	14	6.4	12
Die Grünen[1]				
Repunlikaner	3.9	–	4.9	–
Others	4.3	–	2.6	–
Total seats		204		204
Turnout	68.0		65.9	

Note: 1. In 1990, Die Grüne.

TABLE 7

ELECTION TO THE MECKLENBURG-VORPOMMERN LAND PARLIAMENT 1994 AND 1990

Party	Election 16/10/1994		Election 14/10/1990	
	%	Seats	%	Seats
CSU	37.7	30	38.3	29
SPD	29.5	23	27.0	21
FDP	3.8	–	5.5	4
Bündnis 90/	3.7	–	4.2	–
Die Grünen[1]				
PDS	22.7	18	15.7	12
Others	2.6	–	9.3	–
Total seats		71		66
Turnout	73.1		64.7	

Note: 1. In 1990, Die Grüne.

TABLE 8

ELECTION TO THE THÜRINGEN LAND PARLIAMENT 1994 AND 1990

Party	Election 16/10/1994		Election 14/10/1990	
	%	Seats	%	Seats
CSU	42.6	42	45.4	44
SPD	29.6	29	22.8	21
FDP	3.2	–	9.3	9
Bündnis 90/	4.5	–	6.5	6
Die Grünen[1]				
PDS	16.6	17	9.7	9
Others	3.5	–	6.3	–
Total seats		88		89
Turnout	75.3		71.7	

Note: 1. In 1990, as Neues Forum/Die Grünen/Demokratie Jetzt.

TABLE 9

ELECTION TO THE SAARLAND LAND PARLIAMENT 1994 AND 1990

Party	Election 16/10/1994		Election 21/1/1990	
	%	Seats	%	Seats
CDSU	38.6	21	33.4	18
SPD	49.4	27	54.4	30
FDP	2.1	–	5.6	3
Bündnis 90/ Die Grünen[1]	5.5	3	2.7	–
Others	4.4	–	3.9	–
Total seats		51		51
Turnout	83.5		79.9	

Note: 1. In 1990, Die Grünen.

TABLE 10

ELECTION TO THE BUNDESTAG 1994 AND 1990

Party	Election 16/10/1994		Election 2/12/1990	
	%	Seats	%	Seats
CDU/CSU	41.5	294	43.8	319
SPD	36.4	252	33.5	239
FDP	6.9	47	11.0	79
Bündnis 90/ Die Grünen[1]	7.3	49	5.0	8
PDS	4.4	30	2.4	17
Republikaner	1.9	–	2.1	–
Others	1.6	–	2.2	–
Total seats		672		662
Turnout	79.1		77.8	

Note: 1. In 1990, as Die Grünen in West Germany (3.8 per cent overall; 4.8 per cent in west Germany) and Bündnis 90/Die Grünen in east Germany (1.2 per cent overall; 6.1 per cent in east Germany, which produced 8 seats).

POSTSCRIPT 1995

TABLE 1

RESULTS OF HESSEN LAND ELECTION, 19 FEBRUARY 1995

	1995		1991	
	%	Seats	%	Seats
Turnout	66.6		70.8	
CDU	39.2	45	40.2	46
SPD	38.0	44	40.8	46
FDP	7.4	8	7.4	8
Die Grünen	11.2	13	8.8	10
Others	4.1		2.8	
Total	100	110	100	110

Source: *Süddeutsche Zeitung*, 21 Feb. 1995.

TABLE 2

RESULTS OF NORDRHEIN-WESTFALEN LAND ELECTION, 14 MAY 1995

	1995		1990	
	%	Seats	%	Seats
Turnout	64.1		71.8	
SPD	46.0	108	50.0	123
CDU	37.7	89	36.7	90
FDP	4.0		5.8	14
Die Grünen	10.0	24	5.0	12
Republikaner	0.8		1.8	
Others	1.5		0.7	
Total	100	221	100	239

Source: *Süddeutsche Zeitung*, 16 May 1995.

TABLE 3

RESULTS OF BREMEN LAND ELECTION, 14 MAY 1995

	1995		1991	
	%	Seats	%	Seats
Turnout	68.6		72.2	
SPD	33.4	37	38.8	41
CDU	32.6	37	30.7	32
FDP	3.4		9.5	10
Die Grünen	13.1	14	11.4	11
DVU	2.5		6.2	6
AFB	10.7	12		
PDS	2.4			
Others	1.9		3.4	
Total	100	100	100	100

Source: *Süddeutsche Zeitung*, 16 May 1995.

Notes On Contributors

Jens Bastian is Lecturer in German Political Economy at the London School of Economics and Political Science. He received his Ph.D. from the European University Institute, Florence. He is presently conducting research on comparative labour market policies, and undertaking a study of the implementation of the rule of law in central and eastern Europe.

Bernhard Boll is Lecturer in Political Science at the Martin Luther University, Halle-Wittenberg where he is a member of the research project group on Intermediary Organisations in the new Länder. Recent publications include (with Everhard Holtmann) *Sachsen-Anhalt. Eine politische Landeskunde* (1995) and 'Interest Organisation and Intermediation in the new Länder' in *German Politics* Vol.3 No.1 (1994). He is co-editor (with Rudolf Wildenmann, Andrea Römmele and Albert Somit) of *The Victorious Incumbent – A Threat to Democracy?* (1994).

Wolfgang Gobowski is deputy director of the Federal Press and Information Office of the German government (though his contribution to this volume is made in his private capacity). He was formerly one of the directors of Forschungsgruppe Wahlen, in Mannheim. His numerous publications have been concerned principally with empirical analysis of electoral behaviour.

Michael Eilfort is an adviser to the Christian Democratic parliamentary group in the Baden-Württemberg Landtag. He is the author of *Die Nichtwähler. Wahlenthaltung als Form des Wahlverhaltens* (Schöningh, 1994) and of various articles and reports on the phenomenon of non-voting.

Stephen Padgett is Professor of Politics at the University of Liverpool, chair of the Association for the Study of German Politics and co-editor of *German Politics*. He edited *Parties and Party Systems in the New Germany* (Dartmouth, 1993), and has published widely on parties in Germany.

Peter Pulzer is Gladstone Professor of Government and Public Administration and Fellow of All Souls College, Oxford. He has been Eric Vögelin Visiting Professor at the University of München. His most recent book is *Jews and the German State: the Political History of a Minority*.

Geoffrey K. Roberts is Reader in the Department of Government, University of Manchester. A co-founder of the Association for the Study of

German Politics, his publications have focused upon German and electoral politics. These include: 'The Free Democratic Party in the New Germany', in S. Padgett (ed.), *Parties and Party Systems in the New Germany* (Dartmouth, 1993); 'Extremism in Germany: Sparrows or Avalanche?' in *European Journal of Political Research*, Vol.25 No.4 (1994); 'The Great Escape: the FDP in Superwahljahr' in R. Dalton (ed.), *Germany Votes: 1994* (forthcoming).

Carsten Zelle is a Research Fellow at the Konrad Adenauer Foundation. His dissertation, dealing with the phenomenon of the floating vote in German and the US, has now been published. Previous publications analyse electoral volatility and empirical aspects of German unification.